First Printing, 2025

The Art of Vibe Coding (Let the Creators Create)

Vincent Owens

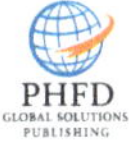

The Art of Vibe Coding (Let the Creators Create)

CONTENTS

Preface

Preface: We Created the Vibe

vibe /vīb/ *noun*

A distinct atmosphere or energy that flows from people, culture, and creation. A pulse felt in rhythm, expression, and innovation. Origin: us.

Let's be clear from the jump: **we created the vibe.**

Before algorithms predicted emotion, we *were* the algorithm—freestyling genius into rhythm, remixing pain into poetry, turning survival into style. We've been designing experiences, translating energy into movement, before tech even knew how to spell interface.

And now, they trying to automate what we *already are.*

But here's the thing—if they gon' code the vibe, they need to know **where it came from.** And more importantly, **we need to know how to code it ourselves.**

This book ain't just a manual. It's a map. A reframe. A revolution.

We're not teaching coding like it's a sterile, abstract thing. We're showing it as what it's always been for us—a form of storytelling. A way to architect the invisible. A portal to systems that reflect who we are instead of rewriting us out the frame.

code /kōd/ *noun & verb*

1. A system of symbols, rules, or instructions used to communicate and build technology.
2. A set of principles or values that guide behavior and solidarity.
3. A cipher. A language. A key.
4. *To be "on code" means to act in alignment with your people, your purpose, and your power.*

This book moves in all those definitions.

We talk code as syntax—yeah. But we also talk about sticking to the code. Living by it. Unlocking it. Not just to get into tech, but to get *free* through it.

Because when you're on code, you're not just playing the game—you're protecting the culture.

When you write code, you're not just giving commands—you're *carving paths.*

And when you break the code, you're not failing—you're learning how to build your own system from scratch.

This is vibe coding.

It's syntax laced with spirit.

It's semicolons with soul.

It's building with intention and culture at the center.

Coding is the new drumbeat. It's the cipher in another language. The future's written in logic, sure—but it flows best when infused with soul. And **vibe coding** is what happens when cultural fluency and technical literacy sit at the same table.

This book breaks down the digital. Deconstructs the gatekeeping. Opens the door so wide your grandma, your little cousin, and your barber can all walk in—and build. Because this ain't just about representation. It's about *reclamation.*

We're building tools rooted in culture, powered by rhythm, and coded in truth.

Because it's not just about learning how to code. It's about remembering that we've always been coding—through language, through style, through community. This is just the next format.

So wherever you start in this book, know this:

You're not just reading. You're entering.

Into a world where your imagination is not only valid—it's necessary.

Where your lens, your lingo, your lived experience is the new standard.

Where you don't just learn the rules—you write them.

Because vibe coding isn't the future.

It's the frequency.

And now? It's yours.

Acknowledgments

I want to extend my heartfelt gratitude to my mastermind group (UniverseCity.Ai), whose insights and encouragement were the spark behind this idea. Your wisdom and support have been invaluable throughout this journey.

To my family (i.e mom dukes) thank you for always encouraging me to dream big and for believing in me every step of the way. To the young readers, whose imagination and curiosity will spark the future, thank you for inspiring us all to keep pushing boundaries and creating new possibilities. And to my future self, thank you for recognizing that now is the time to embrace the moment and make an impact.

CHAPTER 1: From Vision to Vibes –

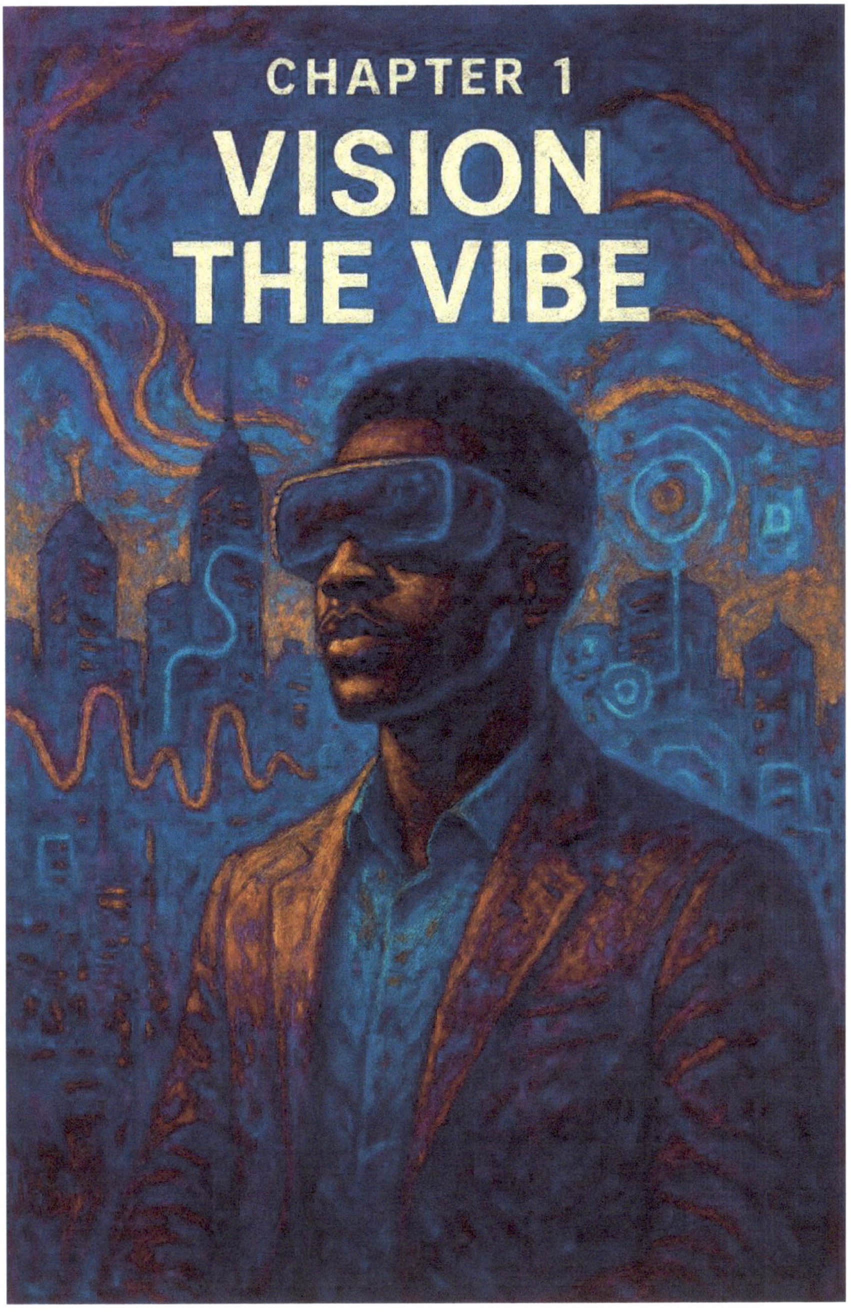
CHAPTER 1
VISION
THE VIBE

Chapter 1 From Vision to Vibes-

You don't always wake up knowing you're about to change your life. Sometimes, it starts with a problem nobody seems interested in solving but you. For me, it was simple—I had a game in my head. A vision. A financial literacy tool that could change lives. Something Black folks could actually use, something our youth could feel, something that made sense. But every time I reached out to a developer, they either flaked or quoted me something outrageous. And the crazy part? Half the time they didn't even deliver.

That's when I realized—I was waiting for someone to build what I was meant to build.

I remember the day I cracked open Replit for the first time. No cape. No magic. Just me, some curiosity, and the willingness to try. It was like hearing a beat drop and not knowing the lyrics yet, but feeling the rhythm in your chest. That's what vibe coding is—it ain't about being perfect. It's about feeling your way through it. About starting where you are and letting your instincts drive.

See, tech tries to convince us that coding is only for the elite, that you need a PhD or a hoodie from Stanford. Nah. I'm from the school of "figure it out." From the neighborhood where creativity was our currency, and problem-solving wasn't a job—it was survival. So when people say, "Vincent, how'd you learn to code?" I tell them, I didn't learn it like a class. I learned it like a hustle.

I started on Replit, then Lovable, then Bolt. I found Cursor, played around with WinSurf, and before long, I wasn't just building my game—I was building belief in myself. And in that process, I realized something powerful: coding wasn't just about logic. It was about vibes.

Energy. Rhythm. Structure. Expression. Just like rap, just like jazz, just like life.

Jay-Z said, "I'm not a businessman, I'm a business, man." That hit different when I started coding. Because suddenly I wasn't just talking ideas—I was building assets. Creating platforms. I stopped pitching and started publishing. I became the builder I was looking for.

Let me tell you something most schools won't: if you can tell a story, you can build an app. If you can organize your thoughts, you can design a system. If you can hold a conversation, you can shape user experience. The gap isn't intelligence—it's access. It's exposure. And vibe coding? It's the bridge.

You see, we don't lack genius. We lack systems that reflect our genius back to us.

And so, vibe coding was born not from textbooks, but from necessity. Not from academia, but from culture. From rap lyrics, late nights, missed deadlines, and kept promises to myself. From not waiting to be chosen. From being the one who chooses.

And the first principle of vibe coding? Let the creators create. That means trust your instincts. Trust your voice. Trust the problem you're called to solve. No one's coming to give you permission.

This ain't about code. This is about ownership. About reclaiming space in tech. About recognizing that the rhythm in your chest is innovation waiting to speak. It starts with a vision—but when you match it with motion, you build momentum. And that's where the vibes begin.

CHAPTER 1: From Vision to Vibes -

The truth is, most people aren't scared of learning—they're scared of feeling stupid. That's why I talk about vibe coding the way I do. It's not some textbook grind. It's intuition mixed with information. You ever freestyle over a beat you ain't heard before? You don't overthink it—you feel your way through it. That's what building apps felt like for me at first.

The first time I tried to make a button work, I stared at the screen for damn near an hour. No lie. But I didn't quit. I Youtubed, I read forums, I asked questions that probably made coders laugh. But I kept showing up. And that's the difference between those who build and those who keep waiting for builders.

One thing I learned quick—you don't have to know everything to get started. You just have to know where to start.

So I tell people, don't wait for permission to be great. Don't wait for someone to hand you the blueprint—start sketching. Make mistakes. Break stuff. That's how the real learning sticks.

You don't learn code. You live it.

That's when I began teaching others. Not as some master, but as someone just a few steps ahead. I'd show them how I broke it down, how I used tools like Bolt to take pieces and remix them into something new. I saw the light go on in people's eyes—not because they saw code, but because they saw themselves in it.

Vibe coding became less about the syntax and more about the story. The energy. It was about creating something that mattered to you. That's what made it stick.

I remember working with this young cat—smart, but he'd been told he wasn't "tech material." He showed me a beat he made on his phone, and I said, "You realize that's sequencing, right? That's logic. That's creativity. You're already a coder—you just haven't translated it yet."

That's why this movement matters. It's not about turning people into programmers. It's about revealing the programmers they already are.

Let the creators create. Let them use their language, their rhythm, their problems to solve. That's how you bridge the digital divide—not with charity, but with clarity. Show people their power and then get out the way.

And yeah, I've had moments of doubt. Times when I thought maybe I was just playing dress-up in a world that wasn't built for me. But each app, each breakthrough, reminded me—I belong here. We all do.

Now when I consult, I tell people this: you don't need to be perfect, you just need to be consistent. Keep tapping in. Keep vibing with the code. Keep building. Because this ain't just about tech—it's about transformation.

It's about turning the impossible into your new normal.

CHAPTER 1: From Vision to Vibes –

There's something sacred about that moment when someone sees themselves differently. Like when a single mother who's never touched a line of code says, "Wait—I could build something for my community?" That's what vibe coding does. It's not just unlocking knowledge—it's unlocking identity. It says: you are not outside of tech. You are tech. You've just been coded out of the equation.

But that's changing.

See, when I started talking about vibe coding, I wasn't just speaking tech—I was speaking to the soul of creativity in the culture. Think about it. Hip-hop didn't wait for permission. It wasn't born in a lab—it was born on turntables, stoops, in parks, with borrowed beats and broken systems. That same energy lives in vibe coding. It says, "We don't need permission to innovate. We innovate because we have to."

Nas once said, "I never sleep, 'cause sleep is the cousin of death." I feel that when I'm up late writing scripts, tweaking interfaces, chasing ideas before they disappear. Because every line of code isn't just a function—it's a freedom. A key to a door someone told us didn't exist.

And it ain't just about the digital—it's about inclusion. Because let's be real: the biggest divide isn't the lack of broadband—it's the lack of belief. Belief that you belong in these rooms. Belief that your ideas are worth building. Vibe coding says, we don't wait for that belief—we build it, one click at a time.

That's why I always tell folks: start with what you feel. If it speaks to your spirit, build around it. If it solves a problem in your life, chances are it can solve it for someone else too. That's what I did with FinLit.

That was my baby. A game, yeah—but more than that, a pathway to understanding money, value, legacy. I wasn't just building an app—I was building a curriculum for the culture.

And I'll be honest—it wasn't always clean. I broke stuff. Lost files. Built ugly. But that's part of the vibe. That's how you know you're in it. You're not watching—you're creating.

And let me tell you something else—they don't teach this in school: tech is rhythm. A pattern. A loop. Just like a drum machine. Once you hear it, feel it, move with it—it becomes second nature. So don't let the syntax scare you. That's just the language. You already speak the vibe.

And when you finally get that first line to run, that "Hello World" to pop up—that's not just code working. That's you working. That's your voice, speaking in a new tongue.

That's the sound of access. That's the birth of belief.

CHAPTER 1: From Vision to Vibes –

When I first started breaking this thing down for others, I realized how much of the fear came from not knowing how to ask the right questions. People didn't think they were smart enough—they just didn't have a map. And that's where vibe coding flips the script. It gives folks a framework rooted in their own experience.

You ever notice how some people light up when they hear something that reflects their world? That's why I always say—we all teach to the clarity of our examples. If you're showing code like it's math class, folks check out. But if you say, "This function is like setting up a verse before the hook hits," now you're speaking a language they understand.

And once they see it—really see it—they can't unsee it. That's where the shift happens.

This is where imagination kicks in. That's the level most people skip over. But not us. Because imagination is the foundation of the value hierarchy.

It's where ideals are conceived, dreams are formed, and vision is cast. This level isn't about just solving problems.

It's about seeing what others miss—feeling the invisible blueprint and daring to build it. Innovation starts there.

That's why I tell folks: protect your vision. Don't let doubt water it down. Don't let people who never built anything question the thing you're building.

Protect your vibe. Protect your process.

And when you're ready to bring that vision to life, structure helps.

That's why I teach people to use what I call the Innovation Picture.

Ten steps to bring an idea into form:

- **First: Vision.** The seed. The reason.
- **Second: Environment**. What space are you building in? Does it support the vibe?
- **Third: Skill set or product**. What are you creating? What do you know?
- **Fourth: Resources.** What's available to help you build?
- **Fifth: Exposure.** Who sees it? Who hears about it?
- **Sixth: Data.** Know your numbers. What's real?
- **Seventh: Customer service.** How does it feel to engage with your build?
- **Eighth: The charge.** What's for sale? What's the offer?
- **Ninth: Don't charge for information**—charge for your time. That's your value.
- **Tenth: Impact**. What changes because of this?

That model came from the grind. From learning what works, what doesn't, and what leaves a lasting impression.

It's not some theory—it's real life, applied through tech.

I once told a young man, "You don't need a team to start. You need a reason." And he took that and ran.

Built an app prototype to help kids read in his neighborhood. He didn't know he could do that before—but he could imagine it.

And that's where it all begins.

Because if we can imagine better, we can build better.

CHAPTER 1: From Vision to Vibes-

I'll never forget the moment I saw a kid light up after debugging his first piece of code. He looked at me and said,

"Yo, this feel like catching my first alley-oop." That's when I knew—we had to change the language around learning.

It wasn't just code. It was confidence. Control. Creation.

This is why vibe coding can't be boxed into traditional tech education. It's not just a method. It's a movement.

A mindset. It's saying, "You already got the rhythm. Now let's turn it into something the world can interact with."

That's also where The Power of the P comes in—Prompt. Because in this new world of AI and automated systems, how you speak to the machine matters.

It's like writing a verse—set the tone, declare the action, know your format, and know your audience. A well-written prompt is the

difference between noise and knowledge. When I teach prompt engineering, I break it down like this:

- Take on the expert persona. Who are you in this moment? Are you a teacher, a coder, a strategist?
- Choose your verb. What's the action? Write, explain, generate, list?
- Set your format and length. Are you building a blog post, a table, a short script?
- Name your objective. What's the end goal of this output?
- Load the prompt with context. Relevant data gives the model direction.

- Tune your style. Your tone and audience should shape the voice of your result.

When you layer that together, you don't just get answers. You get art. You get tailored knowledge. You get power.

And that's what vibe coding is really about. It's not just understanding how to use the tools—it's knowing how to command them with culture.

We're not trying to fit in—we're designing the new standard.

And as I reflect on this journey, from struggling to find coders to building full-fledged platforms,

I realize that every closed door was a redirect toward self-sufficiency. That every no just taught me how to say yes louder—to my vision, to my skills, to my purpose.

Jay-Z said, "A loss ain't a loss, it's a lesson." And that's the energy I carry every time I teach someone to build their first interface or write their first function.

It ain't about turning them into a full-stack developer overnight—it's about turning the lights on. Showing them that the magic is already in them.

They just needed a map. A rhythm. A way in.

And this—this is the way.

CHAPTER 2: Let the Creators Create –

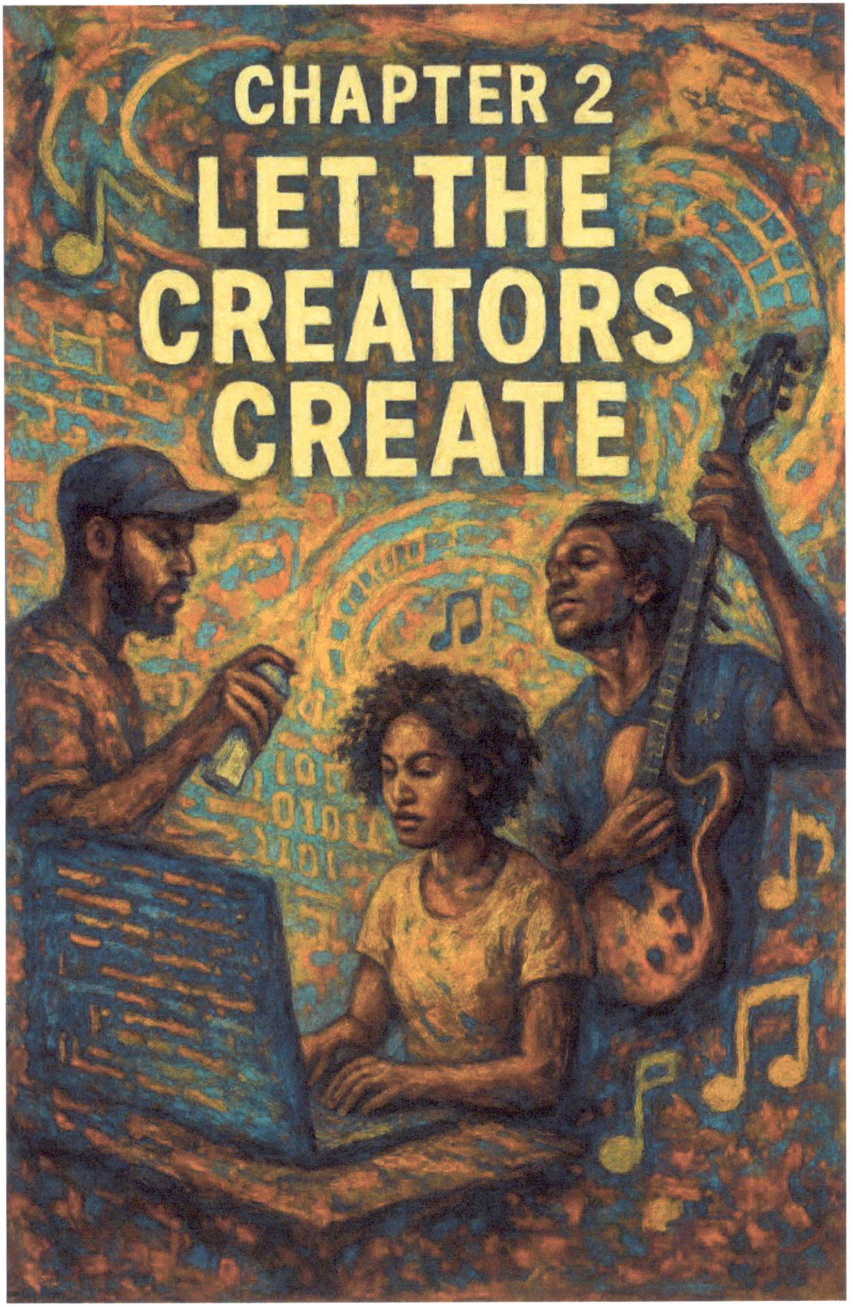
CHAPTER 2
LET THE
CREATORS
CREATE

CHAPTER 2: Let the Creators Create –

Creativity don't need permission. It just needs room to breathe. That's something I had to learn early when I started showing folks how to build. The systems they came from told them "no" before they ever tried. No, you're not technical. No, you're not qualified. No, you didn't go to the right school. But when I watched people; especially the ones counted out—start building anyway, it hit me: you can't stop a creator once they realize they're one.

The world will try to box you in, hand you templates, give you limits dressed up like rules. But the truth is, the most powerful builds come from those who had to hack the system just to survive. And those are the folks vibe coding is made for.

We don't code like the classroom. We code like the cipher.

I've seen cats who couldn't explain HTML turn around and map a full logic flow because they understood how a beat should drop. It's in the rhythm. In the structure of the bars. Future said it best: "I came from nothing, I turned that into something."

That ain't just about the come-up—it's about the creation process. About seeing something where others see void.

When I work with people who never saw themselves as "tech," I watch how their ideas reshape the space. They don't just build—they redesign.

Rethink. Reimagine. And that's why I say: let the creators create.

Stop over-instructing people and start trusting their process. It might not look traditional—but that's the beauty. Innovation never does.

Lil Baby once rapped, "I'm straight as the street, man I came from the pavement." And in that line, there's principle. There's origin.

There's self-made clarity. When folks build from that place, they bring their story into the system. Their pain, their joy, their grind.

That's when the tech starts to feel real.

And I'll be honest—some of the coldest ideas I've ever seen came from people who didn't even know how to label what they were doing.

They just knew the problem and had the courage to create their way through it.

That's why I don't just teach tools—I teach people how to trust their instincts.

If you know how to solve something for yourself, chances are you can solve it for someone else. That's where value lives.

And that's why we need to stop measuring creativity by credentials. Start measuring it by impact. By originality. By soul.

When I hear a young artist tell me, "I just want to make something my people can use," I already know they're on the right path. The tools can come later.

The why is already solid.

So let the creators create. Let them build ugly. Let them break things. Let them remix and reshape and bring culture into the code.

That's how you make something that lasts.

And in the next breath, we'll talk about what happens when that creativity hits structure—and how structure don't have to be a cage. It can be a beat to ride.

CHAPTER 2: Let the Creators Create –

There's this myth that structure kills creativity. But in truth, structure sets creativity free. It's like a beat in a freestyle—you can go anywhere, but the rhythm holds it together. That's how I teach vibe coding. Not as something stiff or robotic, but as freedom with form.

When I first started building apps, I resisted frameworks. I thought they boxed me in. But once I understood them, I realized they were like drum patterns—guides, not cages. They gave me something to push against. Something to flip, remix, rework. That's how creators create. We don't follow—we rewire.

NBA YoungBoy once said, "You can't sit and wait for somebody to feel like you're worth it." That line stuck with me because it applies to everything in this space.

Waiting to be picked. Waiting for someone to fund you. Waiting to be taught. Nah—we move. We make. And in that making, we show our worth.

And that's the power of our communities—we've always created value in places that tried to tell us we had none. Whether it was through music, fashion, hair, language, hustle—we turned scarcity into style. That same instinct lives in tech. We just haven't always known how to channel it.

So when someone says, "I've never built anything before," I say, "That's a lie. You've been building your whole life. You just didn't call it that."

That's why it's so important to shift the language around coding. It's not foreign. It's familiar. It's logic mixed with heart. And once folks see that, they move different. They stop asking for permission. They start producing.

I was at a community workshop one night, showing a group how to prototype using drag-and-drop tools. One of the older guys there—he ran a food truck— looked at the interface and said, “So this is like setting up my morning prep station?” And boom, that was it. He got it.

Because the logic of design was already in him.

He just needed the lens to see it through.

I tell people this all the time: If you’ve ever organized a family reunion, budgeted groceries, styled an outfit, produced a mixtape—you’ve used systems. That’s tech.

That’s logic. That’s vibe.

So let’s stop acting like tech is only for the technical. It’s for the imaginative. The intuitive. The bold.

The creators.

And that’s why we create differently. We move with soul. We write functions with flavor. We design experiences that feel like something. That’s the difference.

That’s the edge.

Because when you let creators create, you don’t just get apps—you get art. You get tools that resonate. You get tech that heals and connects.

And that’s the revolution.

CHAPTER 2: Let the Creators Create –

Sometimes the real challenge isn't teaching code—it's un-teaching doubt. I've seen so many people come into a workshop with their heads down, already convinced they don't belong. They've been programmed by systems that told them tech wasn't for them. That learning stops after school. That creation only happens in Silicon Valley.

But vibe coding is the rebellion to that lie.

It says: if you've ever adapted, if you've ever figured out how to get it done with less, you've been coding your whole life. You've been designing systems. Navigating logic. Solving for x when x kept changing.

This hit me hard when I was working with a brother from Atlanta who had done time and was now trying to rebuild. He told me, "I never touched a computer till last year, but I know how to plan a route, schedule drop-offs, and handle money with no receipts." I said, "You just described logistics, user flow, and inventory management. That's tech."

He looked at me and laughed, but I could see it in his face—he'd never had someone flip the script like that. In that moment, he wasn't an outsider. He was a builder.

And that's why vibe coding can't be taught the way traditional code is. It's not about syntax—it's about connection. The code is secondary. The confidence is primary.

Kendrick Lamar said, "We gon' be alright." And that line rings loud in rooms where the lights are just coming on. Where people are realizing they've had the tools all along—they just needed to see them differently.

So when I say "let the creators create," I'm also saying remove the gatekeepers. Tear down the idea that only certain people get to innovate.

That only certain voices are valid. Because we're not waiting for invites anymore. We're building the room.

And these rooms look different.

In one, it's a girl in Houston designing a budgeting app for her mom. In another, it's a group of teens in Oakland remixing open-source code to track police stops in their neighborhood. In another, it's a DJ using code to trigger lights during live sets.

That's what creation looks like when you let it live.

We don't just build—we bless. We heal. We speak. We shift the culture.

And yeah, it gets messy. But so does every movement that matters.

So stop policing creativity. Stop waiting for credentials. Stop trimming the vision to fit into someone else's frame.

Give people space, tools, and the belief that they can do more than survive—they can shape.

Let the creators create.

CHAPTER 2: Let the Creators Create –

Sometimes, the block to building isn't tools—it's trust. Not in the platform, but in yourself. I've sat with people who had everything they needed—laptop, time, ideas—but froze because they didn't believe they were allowed to make something real. And that's why I keep saying it loud: let the creators create.

We don't need permission slips to build futures.

There's power in believing your story is enough. Your lens is valid. That how you think about a problem is a strength—not a flaw. The world tried to tell us that being different was a weakness. Vibe coding flips that. It says, "Different is the design." That's what makes our apps, our ideas, our systems better.

You look at the most disruptive tech, and it didn't come from following blueprints—it came from breaking the mold.

Lil Baby said, "Started off last week, it was all good / Watchin' me turn up, now she wanna pick." It's that real talk energy. That pivot moment. That transformation. When you go from watching to doing. From consuming to creating. And once that switch flips—it's go time.

And when I teach this, I teach it like music. I don't start with algorithms. I start with expression. I ask, "What's something in your world that you wish worked better?" That's the first prompt. That's the door. And when they walk through, that's when the tech starts to feel like theirs.

I had a student once who just wanted to help his aunt organize her daycare schedule better. He built a drag-and-drop tool using a free template, and by the end, his aunt was running smoother than businesses with payroll systems. That wasn't just tech—that was cultural problem-solving.

And that's the real secret. Most of the problems we're closest to, the ones in our families, our blocks, our everyday lives—those are the richest opportunities for innovation. The market won't tell you that. But the community will.

So I tell creators, start local. Start small. But start.

Because momentum matters more than mastery.

The energy of creation comes from doing, not waiting. You don't need the right title. You don't need the cleanest code. You just need to move. The vibe will follow.

And the beautiful part? Once people see what they can make, they start seeing everything differently. Problems turn into puzzles. Ideas feel more possible. Tech becomes a tool, not a barrier.

And now the vision is alive.

CHAPTER 2: Let the Creators Create –

Creation ain't just a spark—it's a discipline. It's showing up even when the vibe ain't perfect. Because creativity doesn't always feel like magic. Sometimes it feels like work. And that's okay. Because real creators understand that flow follows focus.

That's where a lot of folks get stuck. They think if it's not immediate, it's not meant. But the ones who win? They build through the block. They keep showing up. That's how vibe coding works. It's not about waiting for the stars to align—it's about moving even when they don't.

I always say, the more you create, the clearer your vision becomes. And that's why consistency is power. Every session you code, design, brainstorm—that's sharpening your instincts. That's you becoming.

Symba, that rapper out the Bay, once said, "When you know who you are, you stop chasing validation." That's the whole essence of this chapter. When you create from a place of alignment, not approval, your work hits different. It carries weight. Purpose. Soul.

And soul is what tech has been missing.

I'm not just talking aesthetics—I mean intention. I mean design that feels like it belongs to the people who built it. That speaks their language. That understands their world.

I've seen people build tools in garages, in libraries, in shelters—with no degrees, no networks, no funding—just vision. And when I look at that kind of drive, I know we're in a new era.

An era where the gatekeepers are getting phased out by grassroots genius.

So how do we nurture that? Simple: by normalizing experimentation. By celebrating trying. By creating spaces where messing up isn't a failure—it's feedback.

That's how creators grow.

That's how I grew.

My early builds were clunky. Interfaces janky. Logic half-wrong. But I didn't stop. I shipped. I shared. I iterated. I got feedback and came back sharper. And eventually, those raw builds turned into tools. Those tools turned into opportunities. And those opportunities turned into a platform.

Now I teach this: progress over polish. Don't wait until it's perfect. Make it real.

Because when people feel they can start, they eventually learn how to scale.

And once a creator feels that rhythm—when their imagination meets action and births a result—it's over. They're in. They're changed. They've stepped into authorship over their future.

So this is the message I leave at the end of this chapter:

Start messy. Start scared. Just start.

Let the creators create. And let them build something the world's never seen before—because they finally believe it can come from them.

CHAPTER 3: Black Is Tech –

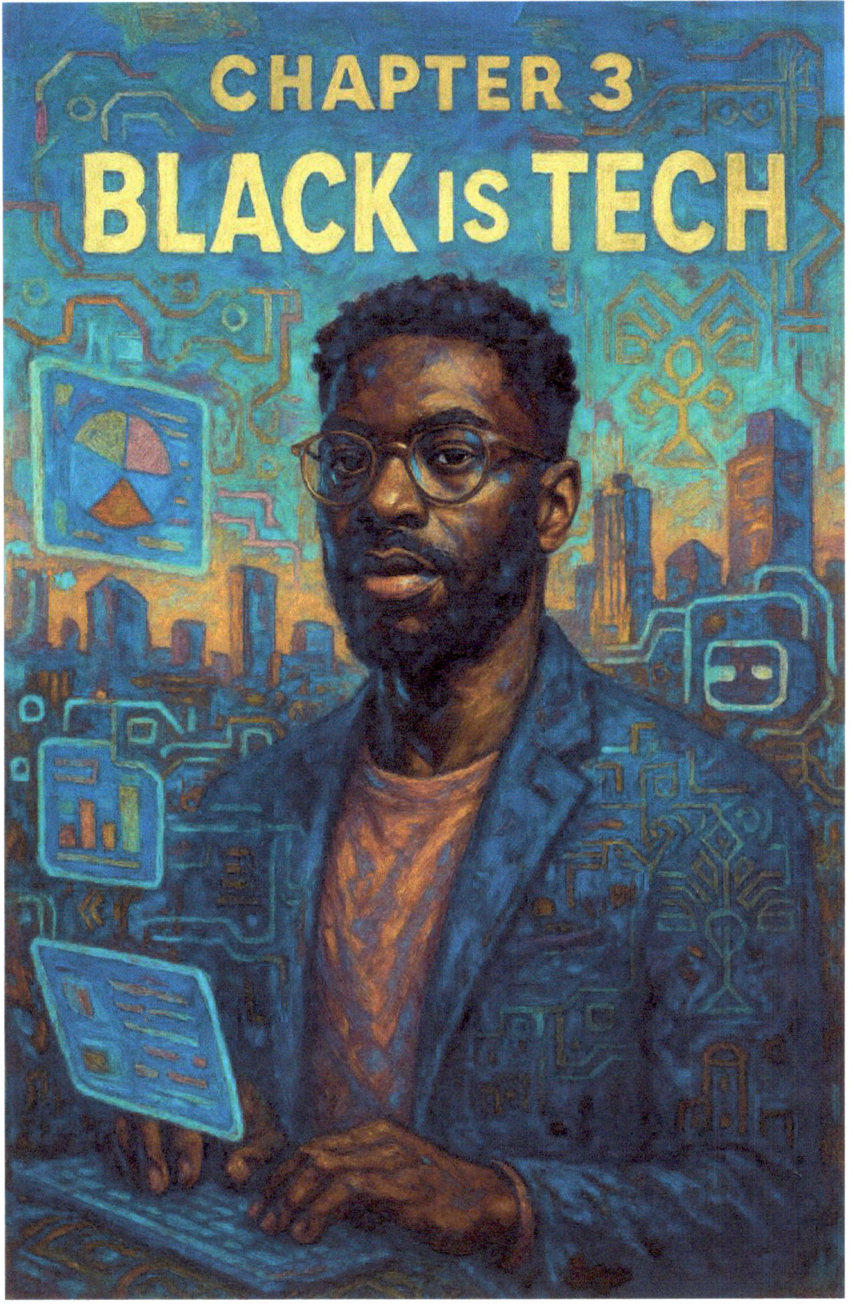
CHAPTER 3
BLACK IS TECH

CHAPTER 3: Black Is Tech –

There's a lie that's been fed to us for decades: that tech looks like hoodies and startups, all white rooms and stock options. But the truth is—Black is tech. Always has been.

From the rhythm in our step to the logic in our hustle, from the creativity we pour into fashion, slang, music, movement—we've always been engineering culture. Vibe coding just names it for what it is: innovation from the ground up.

You ever seen a mama stretch a meal into five different plates and make it work like a system? That's algorithmic thinking. You ever watched a kid flip a broken iPhone into a side hustle? That's product development. We've been building—just not always in ways the mainstream can measure.

So when people say, "Tech isn't for us," I push back with facts. Nah. Tech comes from us.

We don't just consume—we remix, rewire, redefine. And that's why the idea of vibe coding isn't just about bridging gaps in access—it's about recognizing what's already there. The instinct. The ingenuity. The innovation that never got a headline.

I was speaking at a high school not long ago, and I told the students, "Y'all are already engineers. You've just been using your skill set in silence." That classroom got quiet for a second—then one student raised his hand and said, "So you mean my idea for turning sneakers into a delivery app... that's tech?"

I said, "It's not just tech. It's genius."

And this is the kind of reframing that's needed. We don't need to convince Black youth to get into tech—we need to show them they've been in it. That the systems they design to survive, to move, to dream—those are blueprints. They're just waiting to be digitized.

This is about digital inclusion, yes—but more than that, it's about cultural affirmation. It's about showing the kid who codes on borrowed Wi-Fi that he's not behind—he's ahead, because he's building with pressure. With purpose. With heart.

Pusha T said, "If you know, you know." And that line carries weight when we talk about Black tech. Because for too long, it's lived in the margins. Quietly. Brilliantly. Now it's time to bring it to center stage.

Because Black is tech.

Black is logic.

Black is design.

Black is systems.

Black is scale.

And now, the world's about to see what that really looks like.

CHAPTER 3: Black Is Tech –

When we say Black is Tech, we ain't talking metaphors—we talking movement.

Innovation is in our lineage. From Benjamin Banneker's wooden clock to Katherine Johnson calculating trajectories for the moon landing—Black folks have always been technology.

The problem? History classes didn't teach it. The media didn't spotlight it. And the gatekeepers didn't open the doors wide enough.

But the code was always in us.

Tech ain't just typing—it's vision. It's creation. It's the ability to see a need, flip the system, and deliver a new one.

"They want us to download. We're out here uploading truth."

Black culture leads in music, fashion, slang, memes—and yes, in tech too.

It's time we stop showing up as consumers and start showing out as architects.

This is about more than representation. This is about **recognition**. Not just in DEI statements, but in developer tools. Not just in "inclusion panels," but in product design itself.

The apps we use daily reflect pieces of us—yet rarely are we the ones who built them.

That stops now.

The mission? To build like our ancestors hacked systems with quilts, coded survival in hymns, and passed down information in barbershops and back porches.

Now, with LLMs, no-code platforms, and collaborative AI—we ain't asking for a seat at the table.

We're designing the blueprint for a new one.

Because being Black in tech isn't an anomaly.

It's an algorithm for cultural elevation.

CHAPTER 3: Black Is Tech –

There's a reason the most groundbreaking ideas don't always come from the top—they come from those who've had to live in the cracks. And that's why the next wave of innovation isn't coming from tech campuses. It's coming from block parties, from barbershops, from side hustles turned systems.

Because necessity creates innovators.

And when I say Black is tech, I'm not just speaking on culture—I'm speaking on capacity. The raw ability to look at chaos and build order. To take constraints and flip them into features. That's not something you learn in a bootcamp—that's grown in life.

When I teach kids from underserved schools, I don't start with data types. I start with survival stories. I ask, "How did you make it through last month?" One student told me, "I sold water bottles at the park, bought snacks in bulk, then flipped those too." I said, "You built a supply chain. You used profit margin. You optimized a route." He blinked at me like I was speaking another language—but then it clicked. That was his language.

He wasn't learning tech—he was remembering it in a new form.

That's the whole point of vibe coding. Not to teach like traditional systems, but to remind our people that they've been mastering logic and efficiency since day one. We've been coding with culture.

Lil Durk once said, "I come from a block where you can't go unless you got your stripes." That applies here, too. When you've earned your way through struggle, you build with a deeper intent. You don't just code to impress—you code to solve, to save, to shift.

And our shift is overdue.

So what does it look like when Black is centered in tech?

It looks like digital literacy classes that use lyric breakdowns. It looks like design tools being taught through sneaker colorways. It looks like budget apps themed around barbershop talk. It looks like representation—not just on panels, but on product teams.

We don't need to assimilate. We need to amplify.

And that's why this work is spiritual. Not religious, but rooted in truth. It's a reclaiming. A return. A resurrection of brilliance that's been hidden under survival for too long.

Because when we build, we don't just make things work—we make them mean something.

Black is tech.

And tech with soul is the future.

CHAPTER 3: Black Is Tech –

There's a reason Robert Smith—arguably the most successful Black investor in history—says: *"You have to get there fast first... because first matters."*

That isn't just about speed—it's about positioning. In a world where technology moves in exponential curves, the ones who adapt first unlock the real value. And when I say *Black is tech*, I mean we've been doing that—finding the openings, moving first in spaces where survival demanded innovation.

But here's the shift: in AI and Web3, being first doesn't mean being the only winner. As Smith points out, "There can be many winners—but there will be losers." That's the truth of this moment. The people who lean in, experiment, and integrate will thrive. The ones who ignore it won't even have the right to exist in tomorrow's market.

Black is tech because we've always been early adopters—not just of culture, but of systems. We didn't wait for permission to remix a beat into hip-hop. We didn't wait for permission to turn slang into marketing gold. We didn't wait for permission to make fashion statements that billion-dollar brands would later copy. That's first-mover advantage—whether the world acknowledged it or not.

Now, the stakes are higher. Generative AI, blockchain, decentralized platforms—this isn't just about cool apps. It's about control. It's about making sure our communities aren't locked out of the tools that will define the future of ownership, wealth, and creativity.

Robert Smith says his entire portfolio companies are already "100% using code generation, 100% building products, and 100% cutting costs through AI." That's not a prediction—that's the present. Which means our communities have a choice: either watch this wave pass us by, or move like we've always moved—fast, resourceful, first.

And here's the key: first isn't only about money. It's about meaning. When Black is centered in tech, we redefine not just markets but mindsets. We don't just make tools—we make them matter.

So, yes—first matters. But so does culture. So does access. So does the insistence that this revolution doesn't leave us behind.

Black is tech. And in a world of exponential winners, we don't just deserve a seat at the table—we deserve to help write the code that builds the table itself.

CHAPTER 3: Black Is Tech –

When I think about the future of tech, I don't just picture code—I picture culture. Not just lines of Python or JavaScript, but the vibe behind the build. The why. The rhythm. The swag.

Because when Black people get a hold of a medium, we transform it. We don't just use it—we remix it, reinterpret it, and push it somewhere it's never been before.

Hip-hop is a perfect example. Born in the Bronx with nothing but turntables and bars—and now it's a global billion-dollar force. The same's about to happen with tech. Why? Because Black minds + digital tools = unstoppable evolution.

You give a creative from the South Side, or the Ninth Ward, or Crenshaw a platform to build, and they're not just gonna make an app. They're gonna make a movement.

And that's why the stakes are so high.

Digital inclusion ain't just about internet access—it's about equity in invention. If our people aren't building the future, we're bound to be left out of it. That's not fear—that's fact.

But here's the thing—they can't gatekeep the game no more. Tools like Replit, Canva, Figma, GPT, Glide, WinSurf—they're breaking down the walls. No degree? No problem. No investors? Still possible. All you need is intention, imagination, and internet.

And Black creators got all three in abundance.

So the mission now? Shift the perception. Normalize Black tech excellence not as the exception—but the rule.

Lil Baby said, "I ain't changin' my ways, out of time with the wave." That's it. We don't need to conform to fit tech—we need to bend tech to fit our truth. And when we do that? We don't just level up—we level the playing field.

Imagine a world where code is taught through beat loops. Where UI is explained with sneaker designs. Where debugging is likened to freestyle battling—a rhythm, a feel, a moment-to-moment precision. That's not science fiction. That's vibe coding.

And it's happening.

Right now, a single mom in Atlanta is learning to automate her hustle with templates. A kid in Compton is customizing a chatbot to help his homies prep for job interviews. A crew in Philly is building a budgeting app for high schoolers, inspired by house rules.

We're not waiting on tech. We're building it—our way.

And this page? This movement? It's proof that when we lean into our genius, our heritage, our hustle—we don't just participate in the future. We shape it.

If we're gonna truly bridge the digital divide, we need more than access—we need agency. Access means you can use it. Agency means you can own it, shape it, redirect it.

And that's the heartbeat of vibe coding.

Not just giving tech, but turning it into toolkit—for freedom, for legacy, for revolution.

Let's break this down: In most tech spaces, language is the first lock. They throw around acronyms, frameworks, methodologies—and if you don't speak it, they think you can't build it. But we flip that. We speak code in cadence. In cultural rhythm. In metaphors that hit.

We say, "Your data is like your block—you need to know who's on it, how they move, and when to protect it." Boom. Data security. Understood.

We say, "Your API is like your cousin from out of town—he brings stuff you don't have, but y'all gotta speak the same language." Boom. API integration. Understood.

Because we teach to the clarity of our examples.

That's why vibe coding works. It doesn't water down the tech—it lifts up the learner. It meets people with truth. With voice. With value.

And when people feel seen, they show up different. They build bolder. They risk bigger. They dare to own the outcome.

NBA Youngboy once said, "I came straight up out the trenches, everybody around me starved." That's the energy we understand. When you've had to build with scraps, you learn to create diamonds under pressure. And when that same mindset hits digital—oh, it's explosive.

This is why imagination is the foundation of the value hierarchy. It's the birthplace of possibilities. The arena where big ideas are fished from deep water—not shallow sprints.

Ideals are like fish: stay shallow, catch small. Go deep, catch power. It's that simple.

And right now, the depths are calling us.

Tech is no longer optional. It's the new literacy. It's the new capital. It's the new protest. And if we're not building it, someone else is deciding what we deserve from it.

So this chapter ends with a charge:

Let's not just enter tech. Let's redefine it. Reclaim it. Remix it.

Let's build tools that sound like us, feel like us, move like us. Let's train the next generation not just to code, but to vibe—to see their experience as source code, their voice as syntax, their truth as function.

Because when Black is tech,

tech gets soul.

And that's the energy that's gonna shape what's next.

CHAPTER 4: The Power of the P (Prompt) –

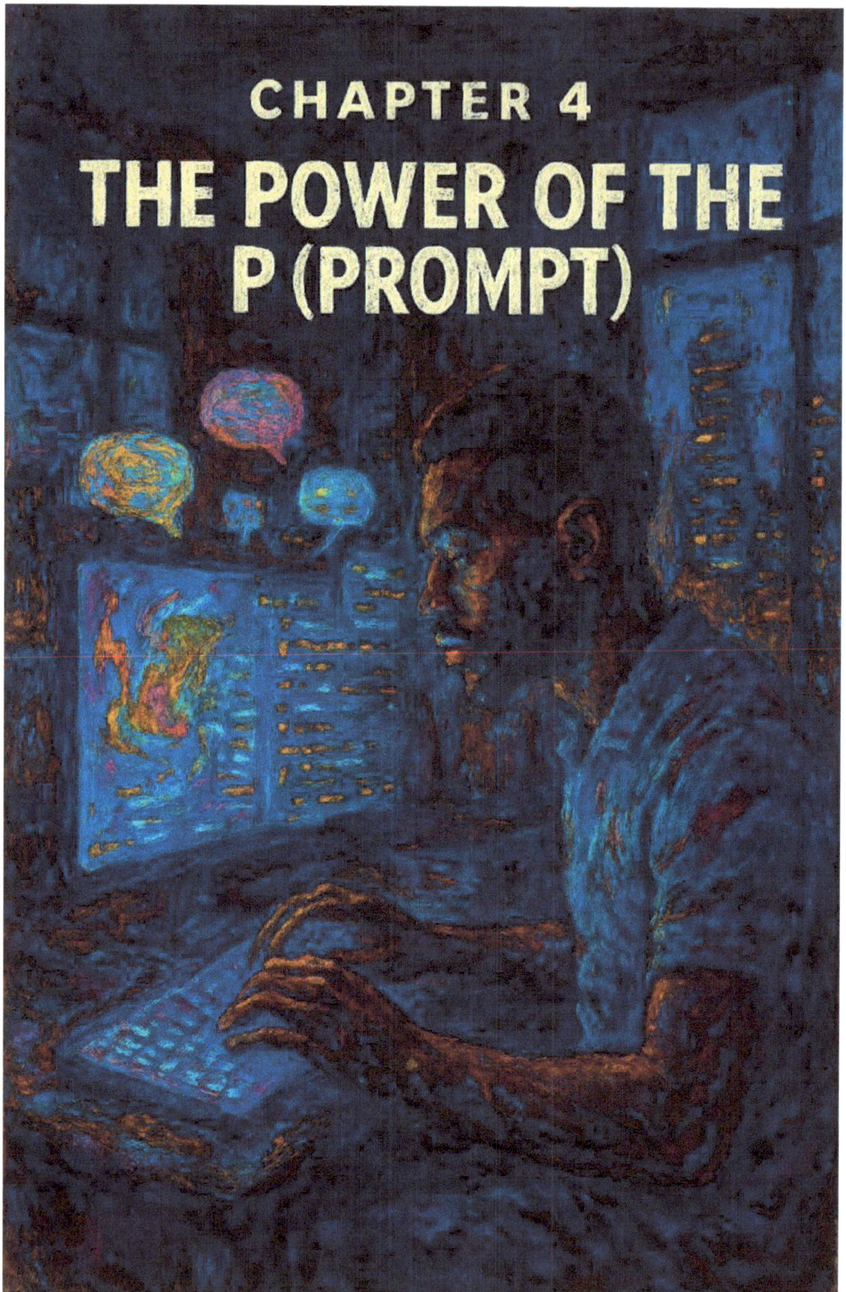

CHAPTER 4
THE POWER OF THE P (PROMPT)

CHAPTER 4: The Power of the P (Prompt) –

It all starts with a prompt.

Not a command. Not a demand. A prompt—a doorway, an invitation, a launchpad. In the world of vibe coding, the prompt is the steering wheel. It's how you navigate the infinite. Because the difference between a genius output and a generic one? Comes down to how you ask.

Prompt engineering is more than typing words into an AI. It's the craft of positioning power.

You gotta approach it like a cipher. Step in with energy, with intent. Don't just ask for a verse—set the tone, define the flow, state the format, and paint the outcome. When you prompt right, the system don't just respond—it resonates.

Let's break down the core elements of a fire prompt:

First, you take on a persona. You don't just ask for advice—you summon the voice of an expert. "You are a brand strategist with ten years of experience in urban culture and digital identity." Boom. Now you're not pulling from a database—you're pulling from perspective.

Second, hit it with a verb. Don't waffle. Command it. Analyze. Compare. Generate. Design. Inspire. The verb tells the system how to move.

Third, be about that format. Let it know what shape you want. A list? A dialogue? A summary? A blueprint? Structure sets expectation.

Fourth, define the objective. Why are we doing this? Who's it for? What's the tone? The outcome? The more the system knows, the more precise it becomes.

Lil Wayne once said, "Real Gs move in silence like lasagna." That's how prompt power works. Quiet precision. Sharp intent. Maximum output.

This is how we bridge the gap between casual use and transformative creation. Because in communities that never got the coding bootcamp, prompt fluency can be the bridge to innovation.

You might not know Python—but if you can prompt, you can build.

You might not understand databases—but if you can prompt, you can design systems.

You might not have the capital—but if you can prompt, you can scale ideas.

This is why we call it the Power of the P. It's not just about tech—it's about framing your future. It's about language as leverage. Expression as engineering.

So when you open up that AI tool, don't ask what it can do. Ask what you can make it become.

Because every word you type is a spell.
And if you cast it right,
it can build your vision into reality.

CHAPTER 4: The Power of the P (Prompt) –

So how do you actually harness the power of a prompt? By understanding **context is king**.

A good prompt ain't just about what you say—it's **how** and **why** you say it.

You're not talking to a genie. You're directing an intelligent partner. The more intention you bring to your language, the clearer your result.

And here's the formula real ones follow:

1. The Persona: Start with "Act as..." Tell the model who it is before it responds. It locks in mindset.

2. The Verb: Tell it what to do—"explain," "build," "summarize," "analyze." Be sharp.

3. The Format: Bullet points? Email? Script? Slide deck? Give it the form.

4. The Objective: Make it clear. What are you trying to walk away with?

5. The Vibe: Specify tone—urban, professional, poetic, concise, analytical. Let it match your audience.

That structure turns you from a dabbler into a digital architect.

"Prompt engineering ain't tech jargon—it's articulation with intention."

And here's the real sauce:

Every great prompt is a **mirror**—it reflects the depth of the one asking.

That's why it's revolutionary when we prompt with culture. When we prompt with real stories. When we prompt not just for function—but for **feeling**.

We stop using AI like a search engine and start using it like a studio.

Every prompt becomes a session. Every output, a rough draft of vision.

The Power of the P isn't just technical. It's **transformational**.

When done right, it don't just spit out answers—it opens up new questions.

And that's how we take back control.

Because when the model understands you? It stops regurgitating data—and starts channeling genius.

CHAPTER 4: The Power of the P (Prompt) –

Before you build anything with your hands, you build it with your mind.

Imagination is the launchpad. The unseen blueprints. The beat before the verse.

It's where we dream not just bigger—but deeper.

They say, "Black people don't do tech." But the truth is, we are tech.

We been innovating before we knew it had a name.

Braiding maps in cornrows. Turning scraps into systems. Beating life out of 808s. Remixing struggle into style. See, tech ain't just about computers.

It's about systems of power—and we've always had the genius to navigate, flip, and build our own. But first—we gotta reclaim imagination. Because that's where code starts: in curiosity.

"Imagination is the foundation of the value hierarchy.

It's where ideals are conceived, dreams are formed, and visions are cast."

This level isn't about algorithms. It's about vision. Innovation is when creativity and intention collide with a need nobody saw coming. You want to vibe code?

Cool. But you won't get far trying to mimic what exists. You gotta see what ain't been built yet. That's what imagination is: pre-visualized architecture.

Like Symba said,

"I had to go deeper. What they see on the surface don't even scratch my real value."

That depth is where big fish live.

We ain't fishing in kiddie pools. We diving into oceans of purpose.

So we flip that concept into the tech space.

If your ideas are small, you'll keep staying shallow.

You want big impact? You gotta dive deep.

Whether it's an app, a system, a prompt, a brand, or a platform—imagination is your currency.

The more vivid your mental picture, the clearer the blueprint becomes. And the cleaner the vibe when the code executes.

Think of some of the most revolutionary apps.

They weren't built by folks asking "What can I copy?"

They were imagined by folks asking "What's missing?"

Now it's your turn.

CHAPTER 4: The Power of the P (Prompt) –

What makes prompt engineering so powerful is how it democratizes creation. It takes what used to require years of coding knowledge or advanced degrees—and makes it accessible to anyone with a vision and a keyboard.

That's why we say vibe coding is for the people. It ain't about gatekeeping—it's about guideposting.

Imagine this: you've got a grandmother in Oakland who's never written a line of code in her life. But she has deep knowledge of her neighborhood, decades of insight, and a heart for helping youth avoid the pitfalls she's seen. She wants to build something—a tool to mentor young women, maybe a daily text-based message of strength, a resource hub, a pathway for connection.

With vibe coding and prompt power, she doesn't need a developer. She can say, "You are a life coach who specializes in empowerment for Black girls aged 13–18. Generate a list of daily affirmations for one month in a conversational tone." That's her blueprint.

The output becomes the seed. And with tools like no-code platforms, she can launch that dream.

It's that real.

And this matters because we've often been told we're users—not builders. Consumers—not creators. But every prompt we write is a strike against that lie.

We teach folks how to frame prompts that reflect them. Their tone. Their flavor. Their urgency.

Symba once rapped, "The difference between a winner and a loser is the mindset." That's what this whole chapter is about. It's not about typing faster. It's about thinking sharper. It's about imagining more clearly. It's about prompting from a place of value and voice.

Because in this new world, your ideas are currency—and your prompts are how you spend it.

So let's flip the script.

Let's stop acting like tech is some exclusive lane.

Let's start treating it like the block. Like the lab. Like the studio.

Somewhere we go to create, to elevate, to document what we see and who we are.

And when we step into that space with full authenticity, when we prompt from where we really live—we don't just get better answers.

We build better systems.

This is the type of knowledge that creates ripple effects. When one person in the community learns how to prompt well, they become a node of power. They teach others. They spark curiosity. They build momentum.

And before you know it, a whole neighborhood is activated. Not by funding or policy—but by prompts. By purpose. By people claiming their role in the future.

CHAPTER 4: The Power of the P (Prompt) –

What makes this movement revolutionary isn't just the use of prompts—it's what we're prompting for. We're not asking AI to write emails. We're asking it to amplify purpose. To solve real-world problems. To unlock pathways our people haven't had access to.

And that intention? That's what separates noise from impact.

Every time someone in a disenfranchised community learns how to write a meaningful prompt, they're no longer waiting for help. They're generating it. They're building the very thing the system was too blind to provide.

And here's the key: it ain't just about being technically accurate—it's about being culturally intuitive.

A prompt like, "Explain financial literacy to a twelve-year-old" hits different than, "You're a community leader in Baltimore explaining why the homie shouldn't spend all his summer job money on sneakers. Break it down in three steps, using examples from rap." That's relevance. That's reach.

We're teaching people to wrap code in culture. To use story as syntax.

That's why vibe coding is so needed right now—because it's not just about learning the tools. It's about learning how to use them in a way that feels like home.

When I built my own journey through Replit, Bolt, and Cursor, I didn't have tech mentors. I had mixtapes. I had ideas. I had too many nights staring at screens, searching for clarity. But each time I learned a new tool, a new prompt structure, it felt like decoding a freestyle—line by line, rhythm by rhythm.

Eventually, I saw what I was doing: I wasn't just building apps. I was building my language into something the machine could understand. And when it started talking back in my dialect? That's when I knew I was onto something special.

LaRussell once said, "I'm proof you can pop without a cosign." That's the energy we bring to prompting.

We're not waiting for someone else to validate our intelligence.

We're not relying on legacy systems to see our genius.

We're building with the tools at hand—and we're making them adapt to us.

And that's the core of this page's lesson:

Prompting is power—but personalized prompting is liberation.

You don't have to change your voice to speak tech.

You just have to know how to aim your truth.

And the deeper your truth, the more powerful your prompt.

CHAPTER 4: The Power of the P (Prompt) –

This is where vibe coding becomes revolutionary—not just technically, but spiritually.

It's the reclamation of voice in a digital world that too often silences nuance. It's the power to shape not only what gets built, but how it sounds, how it feels, and who it speaks to. And that, right there, is sacred.

The final piece of prompt mastery is alignment—aligning your words with your vision, your tone with your truth, your ask with your purpose.

Because sometimes the best prompt isn't the most detailed—it's the most authentic.

It's when you stop performing intelligence and start embodying clarity. When you're not trying to impress the system, but express yourself through it.

That's what makes prompts poetic.

I've seen the most powerful moments come from a line that looks simple on screen, but hits heavy in context.

"You are a freedom dreamer helping a mother in Watts create a schedule that lets her care for her kids and build her business." That's not just an instruction—it's a mission.

Because vibe coding ain't a skill—it's a stance. It's an act of defiance in a system that's still catching up to our brilliance.

CyHi Da Prynce said, "I was taught to never chase the cash, cause the cash gone come when you master your craft." That's real talk when it comes to prompting.

We don't chase outcomes. We craft prompts that call them in.

Whether you're building a chatbot, scripting a video series, or mapping out a startup idea—your prompts are your power. The sharper they are, the more aligned your tech becomes with your culture, your cause, your creation.

And when we teach this in the hood, in barbershops, at rec centers, on Zoom calls with aunties in Mississippi—we're not just teaching tech. We're planting flags.

Flags that say: We belong here. We build here. We run this too.

That's the future we're stepping into—one prompt at a time.

And maybe that's the ultimate message of Chapter Four:

To prompt is to produce.

To prompt is to publish.

To prompt is to participate in the building of a world that knows your name, your slang, your genius.

So write your prompt like a verse.

Stack your format like a beat.

Build your solution like a bar.

And remember—every great shift starts with one well-placed line.

CHAPTER 5: Imagination is Infrastructure —

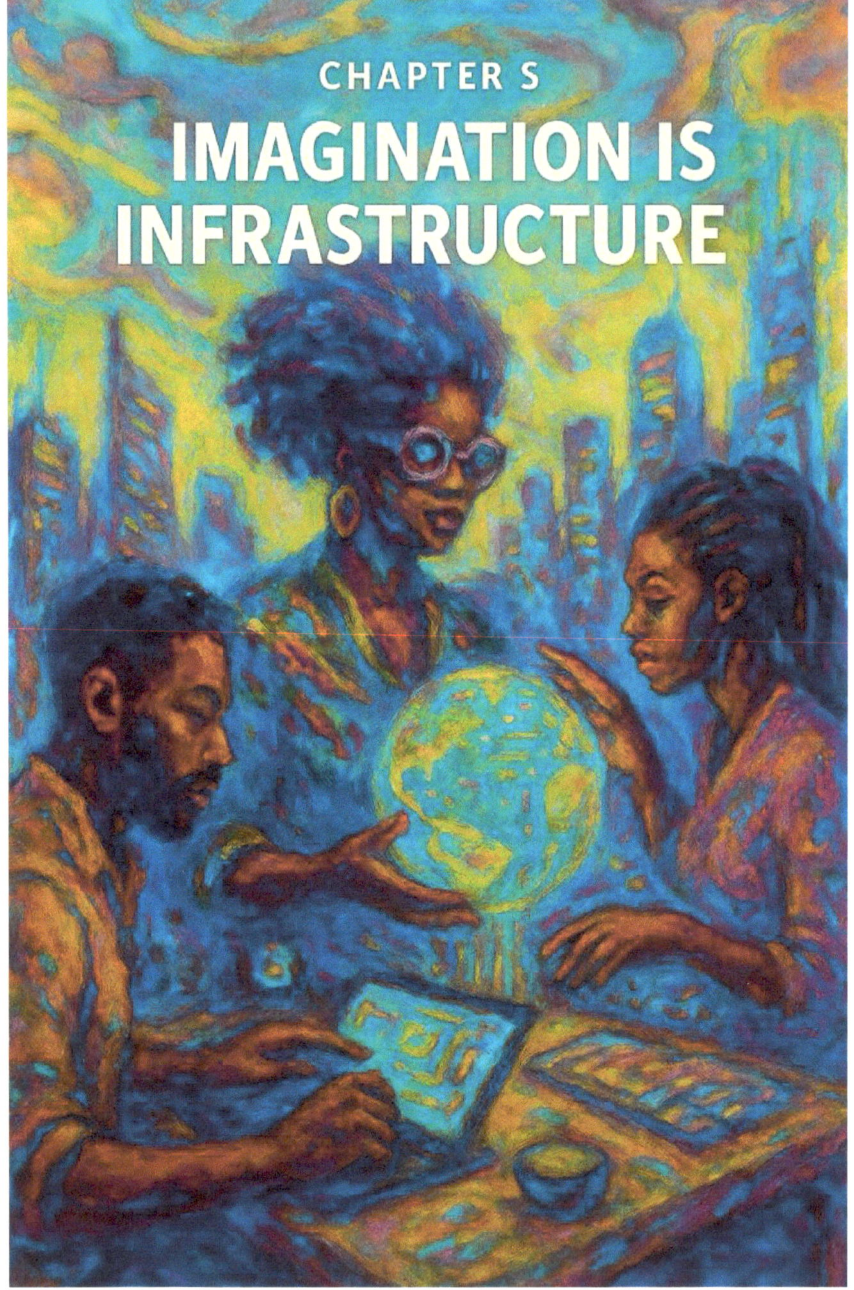
CHAPTER 5
IMAGINATION IS
INFRASTRUCTURE

CHAPTER 5: Imagination is Infrastructure –

Imagination isn't just creativity—it's infrastructure.

It's the base layer. The code before the code. The energy that makes all other structures possible. And for too long, we've been told imagination was optional. That it was soft. Abstract. Something to be left to artists, dreamers, or children.

But in vibe coding, imagination is how we start every build.

Because every app, every prompt, every system—it all begins with an idea that didn't exist until someone pictured it.

We say it like this: "Imagination is the foundation of the value hierarchy."

It's where ideals are conceived. Where dreams are formed. Where visions are cast.

This is the first level of power. Not when the product drops, but when the spark hits. When someone says, "What if..." and starts building from there.

That's the infrastructure we're talking about.

And in communities where tech has always been something built for us—but never by us—this level of imagination becomes revolutionary. Because now we're not just using what's been handed down. We're dreaming up what's been left out.

Let's pause here. In tech, they talk about pipelines, roadmaps, architecture. But what fuels those structures? Imagination. The belief that something unseen can become something essential.

We call it "seeing the unseen and speaking it into the build."

When I was first trying to develop my financial literacy game, I didn't have code. I had an idea. I knew what the game should feel like. I knew how it should move, what it should teach, who it was for.

That vision became the north star.

It's what guided me through Replit, through Lovable, through Cursor. It's what made the tools matter—because I wasn't just experimenting. I was constructing a dream with real utility. A product born from purpose.

So when we teach vibe coding, we don't start with syntax. We start with questions like:

What do you see that no one else does?

What's broken around you that tech could repair?

What would you build if you had no limitations?

Because when the imagination is strong, the tech becomes secondary. Tools change. Platforms evolve. But vision? That travels.

Lil Baby once rapped, "I know what I'm doing, I ain't gotta prove it." That's the kind of self-certainty we need around our imagination.

Not apologizing for dreaming. Not waiting for permission. Not needing a cosign.

Just knowing that your ideas have value—even before they exist.

CHAPTER 5: Imagination is Infrastructure –

In vibe coding, we don't just imagine apps. We imagine possibilities. That's the mindset shift.

Traditional tech often starts with the question, "What can this tool do?" Vibe coding starts with, "What does my community need?" Then we imagine forward.

This imagination-first model is how we reclaim digital space. It's how we build culturally informed solutions from the ground up. Because the truth is, systems aren't broken for us by accident—they were never built with us in mind. So now, we build. But we build from vision—not scarcity.

We teach young coders not to limit their builds to what they think is feasible. We tell them to write out the ideal. Sketch the dream. Prompt the impossible. Because once you can clearly articulate your vision, you can find the tools to get there.

That's why we say: "If you can name it, you can prompt it. If you can prompt it, you can build it." Let's break that down.

Say you imagine a platform that helps kids learn coding while freestyling. You can't code it yet, but you can describe it. That description becomes your prompt. That prompt becomes a prototype. That prototype becomes a real product.

Imagination begets invention. It's why we emphasize imagination as infrastructure—because it's foundational. It's the launchpad for prompts, the seed for tech, and the heart of innovation.

In communities facing digital exclusion, this becomes survival. If you're underfunded, under-resourced, and underrepresented, then imagination is the most powerful asset you have.

Because it costs nothing to dream.

And in dreaming, we blueprint liberation.

Nas said, "I know I can be what I wanna be. If I work hard at it, I'll be where I wanna be." That wasn't just a hook—it was architecture. It was imagination being laid brick by brick into self-belief.

And that's what we teach with vibe coding. That when imagination is clear, focused, and values-driven, it becomes more than wishful thinking—it becomes tech in waiting.

A good imagination describes a world.

A great imagination builds the tools to make that world real.

So we teach creators to lean into the deep end. To go past the obvious. To trust that their perspective matters enough to shape systems, not just survive in them.

Because as we said earlier: Ideals are like fish.

If you want to catch the little ones, you stay in the shallow water.

But if you want to catch the big ones, you've got to go deep.

And down there? The fish are more powerful. More pure.

They're huge. They're abstract. They're beautiful.

CHAPTER 5: Imagination is Infrastructure –

Imagination isn't escapism—it's ecosystem engineering.

When we treat imagination as a utility, something as essential as power or water, we begin to transform our communities. Because at the root of every neighborhood solution, social enterprise, or app that meets people where they are—you'll find a visionary who dared to imagine something different.

And here's the thing: not all imagination looks poetic. Sometimes it looks like frustration. Sometimes it shows up as that moment when you say, "Why hasn't anyone built this yet?" That's your prompt calling.

And we're here to tell you, you are the one to build it.

So let's get tactical.

There's a model we call the Innovation Picture. It frames imagination into a real, structured process. Here's how we break it down:

1. **Vision** – What's the future you're creating? Not just a product—a possibility.
2. **Environment** – Where is this idea going to grow? What context matters?
3. **Identify Skill Set/Product** – What's your idea? And what do you bring to the table?
4. **Identify Resources** – What do you have? What do you need? Who's in your circle?
5. **Exposure** – Who are you learning from? Who's done it before in their own way?
6. **Data** – Know your numbers. What does success look like, and how do you measure it?

7. **Customer Service** – How do you serve? What experience are you creating?

8. **Why/Charge** – What are people really paying for? Your product? Or your story?

9. **Monetization Mindset** – Don't charge for information. Charge for your time.

10. **Impact** – What legacy does this idea leave behind?

Every one of these steps is powered by imagination. And when you work through this lens, you begin to realize that your idea isn't a long-shot—it's a plan waiting on action.

We see this with our students. One young brother from Park Hill had an idea to create a peer-to-peer tutoring app. Not revolutionary on paper, but the way he imagined it—with cultural fluency, gamified incentives, and embedded hip-hop lingo—it was something special.

He started sketching it out. Prompting ideas. Testing flows with no-code platforms. And before long, he had an MVP. And now? He's teaching others how to do the same.

That's why we say we all teach to the clarity of our examples.

Because sometimes it only takes one example to spark imagination in someone else.

This young king didn't start with money or connections. He started with imagination as infrastructure. And then he built from there.

CHAPTER 5: Imagination is Infrastructure –

The power of imagination also lies in its interconnectivity.

When one person imagines something new, it inspires others. But when a community shares that imaginative space—when ideas bounce, combine, and evolve—that's when transformation really takes root.

That's why building spaces for imaginative collaboration is critical.

We've seen it in workshops, think tanks, and community co-creation sessions. When folks realize they don't need to have all the answers—just a piece of the vision—it unlocks the kind of group genius that can birth platforms, businesses, and cultural movements.

That's also where digital inclusion becomes a deeper conversation.

Imagination without access is like talent without opportunity. You can have the wildest, most world-changing ideas—but if you can't reach the tools, the networks, or the bandwidth to build, then the system's still rigged.

We call this the technological disenfranchisement gap. And it's not just a lack of devices—it's a lack of design centered on our realities.

So when we teach imagination as infrastructure, we also teach advocacy.

We encourage folks to demand access, to build partnerships, to be bold in asking for what they need. Because this work doesn't live in a vacuum. It lives in community.

LaRussell said, "I don't need to be discovered—I just need to be connected."

That quote sits at the core of this philosophy.

We're not trying to get put on—we're putting ourselves in position. And once in position, we start to pull others in.

That's how movements form.

We use imagination to build the dream.

We use prompts to translate the dream into systems.

We use community to scale those systems into culture.

And at every level, we remind our people: You are not behind. You are not underqualified. You are not late.

You've just been under-informed.

And now that the information is flowing? The game's wide open.

So as we close in on the final ideas of this chapter, we circle back to this: Imagination is not extra. It's essential. It's not a perk. It's a prerequisite. Whether you're building tech, launching art, designing experiences, or raising kids—you are already imagining the future.

We're just here to help you code it into being.

CHAPTER 5: Imagination is Infrastructure –

So now the question becomes: What will you imagine next?

Because once you understand that imagination is not random—it's rooted—you start to see it as a daily practice. A strategy. A system you can return to whenever you're stuck, or stretched, or just seeking the next step.

We teach this in vibe coding like it's mental push-ups.

Every prompt starts with an image.

Every build starts with a belief.

Every movement starts with someone daring to say, "We could do it differently."

And that's what makes imagination the most undervalued form of resistance.

It's where you plant seeds before systems can suffocate your spirit. It's how you speak joy into blueprints. How you bring rhythm to routines. How you make technology reflect not just efficiency, but soul.

Because if it ain't soulful, it ain't sustainable.

See, we've been trained to code like robots. To create with precision but without passion. That stops here.

Imagination is what brings spirit back into the system.

And spirit is what carries your idea through the grind. It's what reminds you why you're doing this. Why you're showing up to write one more prompt. To fix one more bug. To explain one more concept to the homie that don't even know how to open a new tab.

You do it because your imagination is contagious.

And once your people catch the vision, they start imagining too.

That's how revolutions are born.

Symba once spit, "If they knew better, they'd do better—I'm just tryna educate the game and move better." That's the energy we move with in vibe coding.

We don't hoard knowledge—we spark imagination.

We don't flex builds—we share tools.

We don't wait for the system—we design new systems.

And we do it with flow. With clarity. With power.

So before we close this chapter, here's your challenge:

Take one dream.

Something you've been sitting on.

Something too wild, too abstract, too "out there" for a pitch deck.

Now name it. Prompt it. Build it. Even if it's messy. Even if it's small. Even if it's incomplete. Because imagination isn't about perfection. It's about initiation.

The first line. The first sketch. The first "What if..." And once that spark hits, it's only a matter of time before the build begins.

CHAPTER 6: CODE & CULTURE: THE FUSION OF IDENTITY

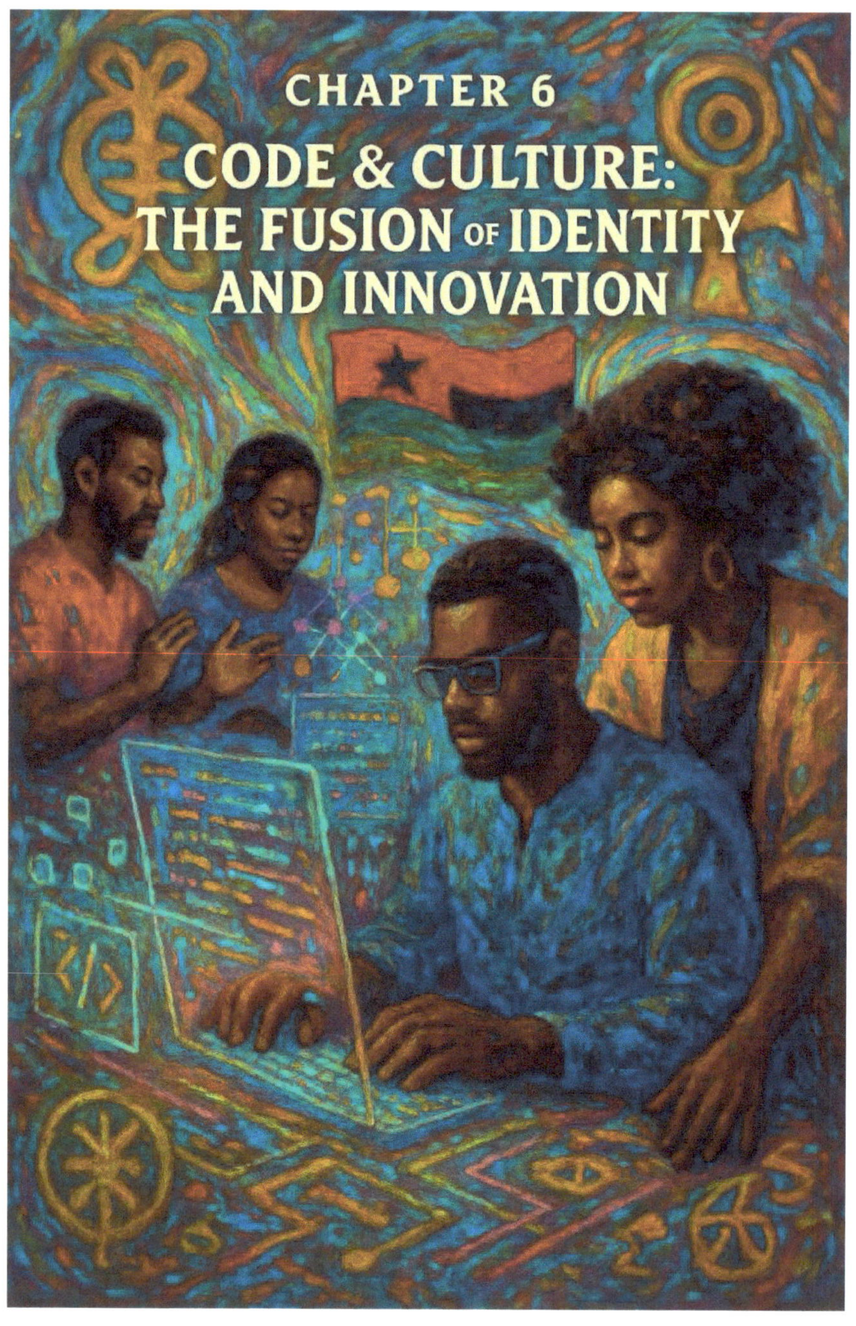
CHAPTER 6
CODE & CULTURE:
THE FUSION OF IDENTITY
AND INNOVATION

CHAPTER 6: CODE & CULTURE: THE FUSION OF IDENTITY

Code has always been culture. It just wasn't always recognized.

From the coded language of the Underground Railroad to the beat patterns of West African drum signals, from hair braiding used to map escape routes to the brilliance embedded in the cipher—our people have always been architects of systems.

We just didn't call it "code."

But that ends here.

In vibe coding, we reclaim that narrative. We show that code isn't limited to lines typed in Silicon Valley. It's rhythm. It's remix. It's reinvention. And it's always been rooted in us.Let's get something straight: What is code?

Code is a language. It's the act of translating knowledge into symbols, patterns, and systems that create meaning and motion.

It's not just syntax on a laptop. It's any design, signal, or story that encodes survival and possibility.

So when you think about the way Black folks invented the traffic light, the folding chair, the automatic elevator door, or the super soaker—we're not new to this. We've always been about that **applied innovation**.

Hair grease? Code. Cornrows used to communicate rebellion? Code. Using rap lyrics to encode generational pain and still bring joy? That's code too.

When we say **Code is Culture**, we're naming a truth that society tried to bury beneath gatekeeping and degrees. We're saying the innovation that moves the culture is just as important—if not more—than what gets printed in a patent.

So let's break the myth: we are not *new* to this.

We are the *original coders of culture.*

The griots? Data storytellers.

The drummers? Communication engineers.

The barbershop debates? Algorithmic logic and ethical processing.

The double-dutchers? Physics in motion.

And in 2025, this history lives on in how we vibe code.

We bring that same creative rigor to our prompts. That same community language to our user flows. That same urgency to make tech that doesn't just solve problems—it speaks our truths.

Roddy Ricch once said, *"I put the new Forgis on the Jeep / I trap until the bloody bottoms is underneath."* That line, metaphorical and coded, reflects both resourcefulness and resilience. It's culture wrapped in a verse.

Because code isn't just about building apps—it's about building liberation.

It's about turning imagination into infrastructure and then into income. It's about using tools not just for clout, but for community repair. It's about coding in our cadence, designing in our dialect, and scaling in our spirit.

So when you hear someone say **Code is Culture**, understand that it's not about fitting in—it's about returning to origin.

We are not guests in this space.

We are the blueprint.

And vibe coding is the language we use to make sure everybody knows it.

CHAPTER 6: CODE & CULTURE: THE FUSION OF IDENTITY

Let's talk about why recognizing **code as culture** is not just symbolic—it's strategic.

Because when you recognize that you come from a lineage of technologists, you stop seeking permission to create. You stop waiting for someone else's platform and start building your own.

This mindset shift matters.

Cose is often taught like a foreign language, and Black folks are too often treated like ESL students in the coding world. But here's the truth: we already speak tech—we just haven't always been taught how to translate our brilliance into the dominant syntax.

That's why vibe coding bridges the gap.

It's not just about tools. It's about translation. Taking the genius that already exists in our communities and aligning it with accessible, digital frameworks.

Because when we talk about building websites, we're also talking about structuring narratives.

When we talk about data models, we're talking about mapping lived experiences.

When we talk about AI, we're talking about turning wisdom into algorithms.

We've always had the wisdom.

Now we're pairing it with the workflow.

And that shift is what opens doors—not just for individuals, but for communities.

Let's bring in Symba again, who said, "You ain't gotta be famous, you just gotta be solid."

That bar is a principle for building. For moving with intention. For focusing less on virality and more on value. That's a core tenet of vibe coding: don't build for hype, build for help.

Because code is culture, when done right, becomes community infrastructure. It's the pop-up app that tracks local water conditions. It's the web tool that lets aunties coordinate meal trains. It's the chatbot that explains financial terms in a tone that feels like home.

It's the remix of knowledge into systems.

And what we're doing isn't just invention—it's reclamation. We're reclaiming code as our own birthright. Reclaiming narrative. Reclaiming access. Reclaiming imagination.

Here's a reminder we drop in every workshop:

The right mindset can develop any skill set.

That means you don't need to know all the code to start coding. You don't need to be a software engineer to architect solutions. You just need the courage to start.

So when you walk into a tech space as a vibe coder, remember:

You're not behind.

You're the beginning.

CHAPTER 6: CODE & CULTURE: THE FUSION OF IDENTITY

One of the most dangerous myths ever told was that Black folks don't innovate—we just imitate.

Let's kill that noise.

From George Washington Carver's botanical breakthroughs to the digital impact of innovators like Lisa Gelobter—who helped develop the technology behind GIFs—we've been the source, not the shadow.

And in vibe coding, we highlight these truths because our narrative is our navigation.

When a young coder sees their history reflected in the systems they're learning, it unlocks something. Confidence. Belonging. That spark of "I can do this too."

And here's why that matters: the tech world doesn't suffer from a lack of talent—it suffers from a lack of cultural context.

See, when developers ignore the lived realities of the communities they serve, they build platforms that feel sterile, inaccessible, or worse—harmful. But when vibe coders step into the scene, we bring our full selves.

We bring cadence. We bring rhythm. We bring soul.

We're building apps that talk like us, think like us, move like us.

And that's a beautiful disruption.

Because now, tech doesn't just look different—it feels different. It resonates.

Like when a student from Atlanta built a budgeting app that used rap metaphors to explain compound interest. Or when a coder from

Baltimore created a mental health chatbot that greets users with, "What's good, fam?" instead of "How can I assist you?"

These moments are not gimmicks—they're cultural fluency.

And cultural fluency is a technical skill.

So we teach our folks how to channel that fluency into UX design. Into prompt engineering. Into logic trees and API flows.

Because when tech reflects our realities, it becomes more accessible. More usable. More transformative.

LaRussell from the Bay once rapped, "I just do what I love and get paid / That's the freedom I been trying to make."

And that right there? That's the goal.

To use vibe coding not just as a career move, but as a liberation tool.

We're not just chasing funding rounds—we're chasing freedom rounds. Where every app, every build, every system serves the people who've historically been left out.

Black isn't a "user persona."

Black is the design genius.

CHAPTER 6: CODE & CULTURE: THE FUSION OF IDENTITY

Let's take it further—beyond just visibility and into viability.

If Black is tech, then our communities deserve not just recognition in the digital economy but equity in it. That means seats at the table, and also the blueprints for building our own tables from scratch. It's not about assimilation. It's about ownership.

Vibe coding is the toolkit for this movement.

It gives us the framework to move from idea to impact without needing a CS degree or a million-dollar investment. And it's in that accessibility where we find our power.

Remember this: Ideals are like fish. If you want to catch the little fish, stay in the shallow water. But if you want to catch the big fish, you gotta go deeper. That's imagination at work. That's vision requiring courage.

And courage is what turns code into a cultural weapon.

We've seen youth in Oakland use vibe coding to create platforms that document community stories. Not for likes, but for legacy. They're preserving oral traditions in digital form, remixing family history into searchable archives, and building family trees with code.

That's tech. That's ancestral memory meeting machine learning.

This is what happens when we flip the narrative.

Instead of asking, "How can we fit into tech?"

We ask, "How can tech fit into us?"

We use the culture as context, the block as a blueprint.

And every time we do, we shift the landscape.

Enter the words of Mick Jenkins: "Drink more water, or you might die."

Simple. But layered.

That quote, metaphorically, reminds us to nourish ourselves with what sustains growth—information, creativity, and community. If you don't feed your curiosity, your craft, and your connection to culture, you starve your potential.

In vibe coding, this is critical. We feed each other. We water each other's ideas.

We treat every prompt like a seed and every build like a harvest.

And most importantly—we share the harvest.

Because gatekeeping is the antithesis of innovation.

True innovation is abundant. Communal. Collaborative.

So as we approach the final stretch of this chapter, the message is this:

Black is tech.

Black is the architect.

Black is the algorithm.

CHAPTER 6:CODE & CULTURE: THE FUSION OF IDENTITY A

So where do we go from here?

If **code is culture**, then our future must reflect that truth.

It means more than access—it means agency. It's not just about being allowed into the digital economy. It's about shaping it. Owning it. Innovating it on our own terms.

That's what vibe coding is really about.

It's about rewriting the blueprint of tech to include not just equity, but expression. It's about telling young creators, "You don't have to change who you are to fit into this world—you can make the world fit around you."

We want kids from the South Side and South Central to see themselves not just as users but as builders.

We want elders to see that their wisdom can be systematized. That their knowledge—passed down through stories, rituals, rhythms—can live on in apps, automations, and interfaces.

That's what the **New Principles of Code as Culture** are all about:

1. **Vision** – define the change you want to see.
2. **Environment** – build spaces where creativity is safe and supported.
3. **Identity & Skill** – align your strengths with tools that amplify them.
4. **Resources** – gather people, platforms, and funding with intention.
5. **Exposure** – share your work, test it, let it be seen.
6. **Numbers** – know your data, measure impact, iterate with clarity.
7. **Service** – design with empathy and community in mind.
8. **Value** – be clear on what's being offered, and why it matters.
9. **Worth** – don't devalue your knowledge; price your time, not just information.
10. **Impact** – ensure the work creates lasting transformation.

This isn't just a strategy. It's a survival plan. A liberation framework. A legacy structure.

We've watched people use vibe coding to level up their side hustles, turn community initiatives into scalable solutions, and build tech not for validation—but for value.

The difference between problem solvers and solution seekers is key.

Problem solvers get stuck analyzing the issue.

Solution seekers move forward. They test, they tweak, they build again.

We need more solution seekers.

And we need to protect our imagination at all costs, because imagination is the foundation of the value hierarchy. It's where ideals are conceived, dreams are formed, and visions are cast.

So if you're still wondering if **code really is culture**, let this be your reminder:

You've been coding.

Your community has been coding.

Your creativity has always been a form of engineering.

Let's close this chapter with a quote from Joey Bada$$:

"The only time you should look down on someone is when you're helping them up."

That's the ethic of vibe coding.

We don't just build for ourselves—we build for and with our people.

Now imagine what happens when the whole block starts building.

CHAPTER 7: Code Switching the System –

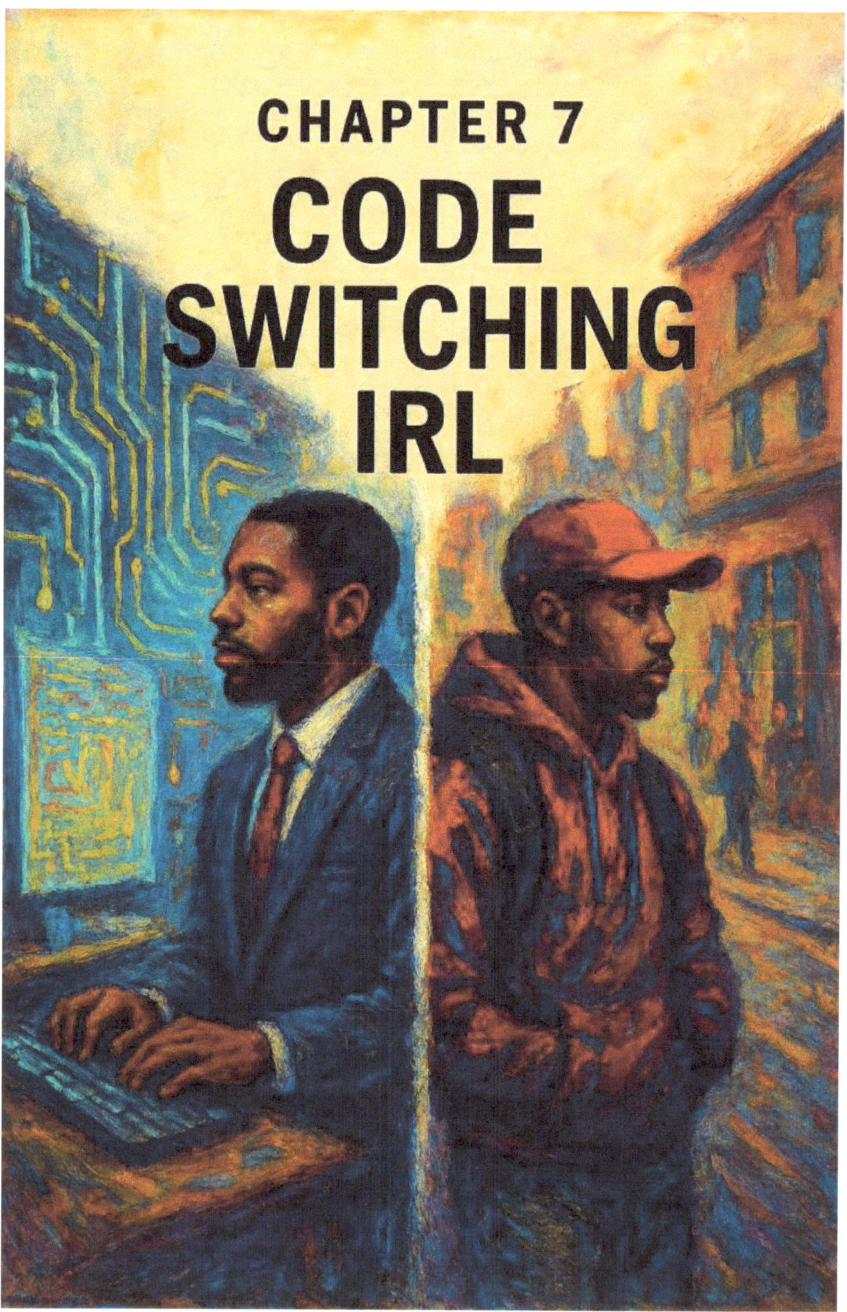
CHAPTER 7
CODE SWITCHING IRL

CHAPTER 7: Code Switching the System

Code-switching has always been our software.

Long before tech caught up, we were switching codes—linguistic, cultural, behavioral—just to navigate spaces that weren't designed for us. In boardrooms, classrooms, courtrooms. And now, we're doing it in algorithms.

But here's the flip: we're not just switching anymore—we're scripting.

We're writing the new rules.

See, vibe coding teaches us that the same language we were told to hide is now the language that can train machines. The way we talk, the rhythm in our words, the metaphors and flow—all of that is data. Valuable data. And it belongs in these systems.

Let's talk about AAVE—African American Vernacular English.

It's more than slang. It's a structure. A system of communication rooted in resistance, rhythm, and realness. And if AI doesn't understand AAVE, it doesn't understand a whole world of people.

That's why vibe coding is revolutionary. It's not just about getting tech to talk to us—it's about teaching tech to understand us.

Because when we prompt these models, we're not just feeding commands—we're feeding culture. Every phrase we use, every analogy, every custom-tailored prompt is teaching the model: this is our language, and it's valid.

Think about it. We've been told to "talk proper" to be understood. But what happens when the systems learn to meet us where we are?

When the paradigm change, the culture is going to change.

That quote ain't just a bar—it's a blueprint. Paradigms shift when new patterns get recognized. When you train a model to recognize your pattern—your way of speaking, your style of thinking—you're shifting the paradigm.

And once that happens? The culture evolves.

It means young coders won't have to mimic Silicon Valley lingo just to be taken seriously.

It means you can say "run me a breakdown" instead of "summarize this text" and still get top-tier output.

It means your dialect is respected—not corrected.

That's the magic of code-switching the system.

We're not just adapting to tech.

We're making tech adapt to us.

CHAPTER 7: Code-Switching the System –

Let's be real: the moment we realize that language is a form of programming, the whole world opens up.

Because when we say "code-switching," it's not just about changing how we speak—it's about changing how we're heard.

And vibe coding flips the power dynamic. Instead of changing ourselves to fit the system, we change the system to fit our voice.

This shift is cultural. This shift is technological.

Because what's code if not language with rules? And what's language if not culture in motion?

We've always had the rhythm. The remix. The ability to break down complex ideas into slick metaphors, tight bars, layered double entendres. And now, we're channeling that energy into technical fluency.

Think about it—when an AI model is trained only on one type of grammar, tone, or dialect, it misses the entire human experience. It becomes exclusive. Incomplete. Biased by design.

But when you start teaching that model AAVE, local slang, regional phrases, or just the flavor of how we talk? You're not dumbing it down—you're leveling it up.

This is what code-switching the system is really about.

It's about building technology that mirrors the people who use it—not erases them.

So when a vibe coder sits down to build, they don't start with code syntax—they start with cultural syntax. They start with what makes people feel seen, heard, and honored. And from there, they write prompts, build automations, design flows.

You ever notice how a good beat matches your vibe without needing explanation? That's how tech should feel—like it knows you already.

Like when Lil Baby said, "I made a promise, I was never gon' fold."

That's a vow we carry into this work.

We promise to build systems that don't fold under pressure. That don't fold under bias. That don't fold when asked to understand the communities we serve.

We build with integrity. With clarity. With soul.

Because if you can code-switch, you can design.

If you can write a bar that makes somebody say "whew!"—you can write a prompt that builds a whole process.

So let's teach the next wave not just how to fit into tech—but how to make tech fit into them.

And let's remind every coder of color: your language is valid. Your rhythm is valid. Your thoughts are worth scripting.

We're not just switching codes.

We're setting new ones.

CHAPTER 7: Code-Switching the System –

It's time we go even deeper.

Code-switching, at its core, is survival. It's a life skill born out of necessity—an ability to adapt quickly, read the room, adjust your tone, shift your slang, flip your posture. It's how we've navigated oppressive systems with grace and grit.

But now, it's becoming something else: a creative superpower.

When we apply that adaptability to language models, automation flows, and design systems, we're building with a new form of fluency. It's not just multilingual—it's multi-dimensional.

You can teach a bot how to speak like the barbershop.

You can build an app that feels like a Friday night on Crenshaw.

You can prompt in a way that hits like a mixtape intro.

This is coding on our terms.

And the beauty of it? It's scalable.

We've had folks go from not knowing a single line of code to developing chatbots for community organizers—bots that use casual, authentic language to walk users through voter registration or financial literacy. That's vibe coding. That's what happens when you stop forcing people to "speak tech" and start teaching tech to speak people.

Every prompt becomes a story.

Every loop is a memory.

Every output is a reflection of the culture that built it.

We're in a new era of digital storytelling—and Black folks are its most seasoned narrators.

Let's look at another angle: education.

What happens when we use code-switching as a method to teach tech concepts?

Suddenly, metaphors matter more than mechanics.

We explain data types like hair textures.

We break down loops using double-dutch rhythms.

We model APIs like block parties—everyone contributing something unique to the flow.

This approach doesn't dilute the knowledge. It deepens the connection.

And that's what makes vibe coding sustainable. It meets learners where they are and gives them the confidence to teach it back. That's real impact.

As Nipsey Hussle said, "Luck is just bein' prepared at all times, so when the door opens you're ready."

That quote speaks directly to the system. To the gatekeepers. To the traditionalists who think tech can only be taught one way. It challenges them to rethink how intelligence shows up—and who it belongs to.

Because we're not waiting for recognition anymore.

We're building with our voices, our roots, our rules.

CHAPTER 7: Code-Switching the System –

Let's build on it.

Once you start training systems to understand your world, you begin to see just how many of our narratives never made it into the datasets. They weren't excluded by accident—they were excluded by design. But we're flipping that design now.

Through vibe coding, we are injecting culture, resilience, and rhythm into codebases that have long been cold, corporate, and sterile.

This isn't just about representation—it's about reprogramming the pipeline.

And when we talk about tech innovation from the block, let's not forget figures like Idris Sandu, the tech visionary behind Nipsey Hussle's smart store. He once said, "I'm not a technologist. I'm a cultural architect." That's exactly what vibe coders are becoming.

We're not just solving problems—we're designing futures.

With every prompt we craft, we're shaping how AI interacts with us. With every low-code tool we tap into, we're bridging that gap between imagination and execution. Because vibe coding isn't about learning a programming language. It's about making tech speak your truth.

We're building tools that reflect our memories, our values, and our block.

Imagine a scheduling tool that talks to you like your cousin does.

Or an AI mentor that knows you're balancing work, school, and a side hustle.

Or an app that teaches credit repair in your dialect with the flavor of your favorite playlist.

This is what happens when we stop gatekeeping code and start democratizing tech through culture.

And don't think this is only for the young folks. OGs in the community are stepping into vibe coding with a spirit of entrepreneurship. They're using it to automate outreach, track community engagement, or digitize decades of wisdom passed down through barbershop chairs and church pews.

Larry June put it plain: "Numbers don't lie, but people do."

So we build tech that centers real people, not just data points. That's the difference.

We're not trying to replace the human—we're trying to enhance the human experience through culturally aligned technology. And that's what vibe coding unlocks.

It gives us agency. Voice. Vision.

And most of all—it gives us a lane to build our own future without asking for permission.

Let's land the plane.

What we're doing with vibe coding isn't just technical work—it's cultural preservation. It's empowerment. It's legacy-building.

And the wild part? It's just the beginning.

We're still scratching the surface of what it means to bring our whole selves into tech—not watered down, not whitewashed, not sanitized for corporate comfort. But raw. Creative. Bold.

A wise man once said: "I'm always being me. That's how I make my bread."

That authenticity? That's currency in the vibe coding world.

When we talk about "code-switching the system," it's not just about adapting language—it's about transforming entire structures. Making room for imagination, for rhythm, for spirit.

Because the truth is, every cultural movement in history had a soundtrack, a style, and a system.

This one? Vibe coding is the system. The new curriculum. The new economy. The new vibe.

We're moving from asking, "Can I be part of this tech world?" to stating, "This is the tech world—we just brought the sauce."

We need to make sure the next generation grows up knowing they're not visitors to the digital economy—they're architects of it. They're not waiting on invites. They're designing the whole venue.

And it all starts with language. With owning our rhythm. With understanding that if we can narrate a life, we can narrate a program.

This means training AI to not just process Black speech, but to honor its tone, intent, nuance, and context. It means embedding our stories into the datasets that guide the next generation of digital tools.

It means making sure when someone from our community opens a no-code app, it doesn't feel like a foreign planet—it feels like home.

A place where your lingo ain't lost in translation.

Where your goals are understood, not questioned.

Where your hustle is seen as innovation, not survival.

Because let's be clear: our creativity has always been tech.

From stacking crates to build a hoop, to reworking a gospel loop into a platinum record—our people been engineering. Been innovating. Been hacking systems to work for us.

Now, with vibe coding, we finally have a language and a platform that lets us do it with power, pride, and precision.

So as we wrap this chapter, let this be the call to action:

Stop waiting to be taught how to build.

Start using what you already know.

Start speaking your world into code.

Because when you switch codes, you don't just enter new rooms.

You open new doors.

CHAPTER 7: Code-Switching the System –

Code switching was once a survival skill.

Now—it's strategy.

We used to change how we spoke to get by.

Now, we're changing how systems speak so we can thrive.

This page is about bringing it full circle.

Not just recognizing that our voice has power—but making sure it's part of the infrastructure.

See, vibe coding isn't about fitting in. It's about making the system flex for us.

When we switch codes now, it ain't for approval—it's for optimization.

Let's get real: language models weren't trained to understand us.

But now we have the power to prompt, train, tune, and tweak them.

And what do we feed them?

Our vibe.

Our flow.

Our syntax.

That's how we flip it.

We're not asking the system to translate us anymore.

We're teaching the system to speak our truth.

Let's say you're a young dev in Baltimore. You grew up around rhythm and hustle.

You know how to get a point across in half the words, with double the meaning.

That's a skill.

And when you bring that skill into your code?

You're not just coding—you're composing.

Just like the block taught us to read a room, vibe coding teaches us to read the model.

To know what it needs to give the output we envision.

And we don't need to change our language—we just need to map it to power.

So what's the takeaway from this chapter?

~Your dialect is data.

~Your slang is syntax.

~Your perspective is the prompt.

When we bring all of that into vibe coding, we don't just improve the model—we redefine it.

LaRussell said, "I used to think I needed a label. Then I realized—I am the platform."

That's what this chapter is really about.

We are the interface.

We are the new input.

And now, we're building output that feels like us.

So let the model learn your language.

Let the system adapt to your swag.

Let your prompts teach the next coder what authenticity looks like in the digital world.

Because in this new era, we don't code to fit in.

We vibe to stand out.

CHAPTER 8: Architects of Innovation –

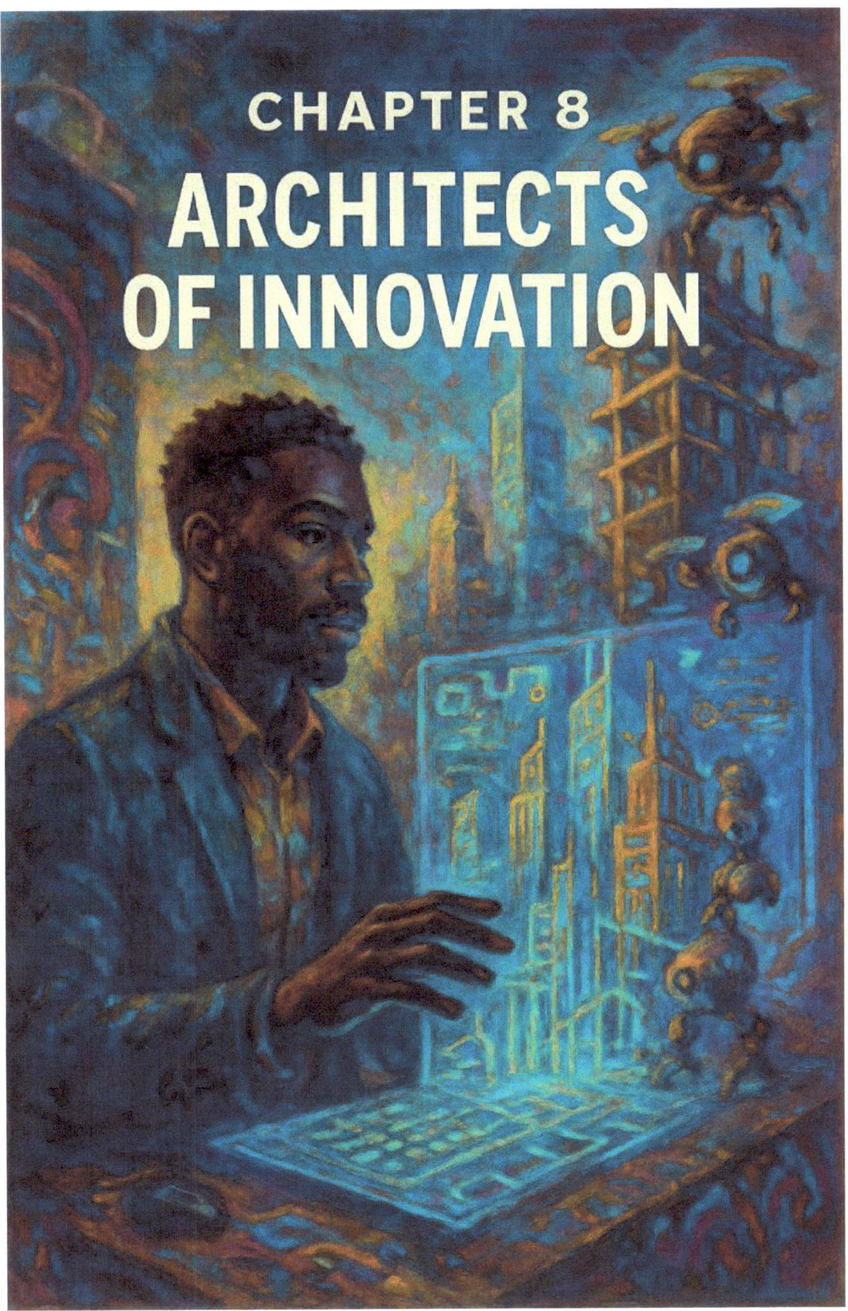
CHAPTER 8
ARCHITECTS
OF INNOVATION

CHAPTER 8: Architects of Innovation –

Before you build anything with your hands, you build it with your mind.

Imagination is the launchpad. The unseen blueprints. The beat before the verse.

It's where we dream not just bigger—but deeper.

They say, "Black people don't do tech." But the truth is, we are tech.

We been innovating before we knew it had a name.

Braiding maps in cornrows. Turning scraps into systems. Beating life out of 808s. Remixing struggle into style.

See, tech ain't just about computers.

It's about systems of power—and we've always had the genius to navigate, flip, and build our own.

But first—we gotta reclaim imagination.

Because that's where code starts: in curiosity.

"Imagination is the foundation of the value hierarchy.

It's where ideals are conceived, dreams are formed, and visions are cast."- Vincent Owens

This level isn't about algorithms. It's about vision.

Innovation is when creativity and intention collide with a need nobody saw coming.

You want to vibe code?

Cool. But you won't get far trying to mimic what exists.

You gotta see what ain't been built yet.

That's what imagination is: pre-visualized architecture.

Like Symba said, "I had to go deeper. What they see on the surface don't even scratch my real value."

That depth is where big fish live.

We ain't fishing in kiddie pools. We diving into oceans of purpose.

So we flip that concept into the tech space.

If your ideas are small, you'll keep staying shallow.

You want big impact? You gotta dive deep.

Whether it's an app, a system, a prompt, a brand, or a platform—imagination is your currency.

The more vivid your mental picture, the clearer the blueprint becomes. And the cleaner the vibe when the code executes.

Think of some of the most revolutionary apps.

They weren't built by folks asking "What can I copy?"

They were imagined by folks asking "What's missing?"

Now it's your turn.

CHAPTER 8: Architects of Innovation –

The problem ain't lack of intelligence—it's lack of imagination applied.

In our neighborhoods, you'll find architects of strategy, designers of systems, and masters of game theory who've never sat in a tech conference or touched a dev bootcamp.

That chess board on the corner? That's logic.

That hustle blueprint? That's systems thinking.

That freestyle? That's rapid ideation with creative syntax.

The only thing separating the block from the boardroom is translation. And vibe coding is that translation tool.

It lets us take the culture—the rhythm, the dialect, the spirit—and plug it into these platforms that were never built with us in mind. That's why imagination ain't a soft skill—it's survival. And it's time we treat it like the superpower it is.

"The right mindset can develop any skill set".

There's a difference between problem solvers and solution seekers.

I always say "Problem solvers focus on the problem. Solution seekers focus on the solution."

Think about that next time you run into a bug in your idea. Don't just analyze what's wrong. Imagine what's right—and build toward that.

This is why prompt engineering became a game changer. When you combine imagination with language and tone, you don't just ask AI for help—you guide it with vision.

Now let's talk value hierarchy. At the top? Imagination.

Not execution. Not even knowledge. Because all of that follows what you can first conceive.

And here's the secret: imagination is free. It don't cost nothing to dream.

But the system don't reward dreamers unless they build.

That's why this chapter isn't just poetic—it's strategic.

If you don't imagine new systems, you'll stay plugged into someone else's.

If you don't visualize equity, you'll keep inheriting poverty.

And if you don't create your own prompts, someone else will code your reality.

So, write your own script.

We used to freestyle because we had no beats.

Now we build apps because we got the beats, the blueprint, and the bandwidth. Welcome to the new level.

CHAPTER 8: Architects of Innovation—

Just know imagination is the origin, but execution is the ritual.

You don't just imagine your way into new systems—you manifest them through movement.

But here's the twist: when the imagination is strong, execution becomes less grind and more groove.

It's like jazz.

You set the structure. Then you improvise inside it.

You don't need to write every note—just vibe with the rhythm you built.

And that's what makes vibe coding different from traditional dev paths.

It respects the feel, not just the function.

You might not know Python, but you know pattern.

You might not write in Java, but you speak fluency in flow.

So when you start imagining an app or a tool or a prompt, you don't have to start with syntax.

Start with a sentence. A sketch. A sound. A feeling.

Then bring it into the world with platforms that do the heavy lifting:

Replit, Glide, Bubble, Wized, Bolt, Xano, Zapier—they ain't just apps.

They're the new notebooks. The new canvases. The new MPCs.

And in the middle of this creative tech?

You, with your ideas that came from lived experience.

"Ideals are like fish. If you want to catch the little fish, you can stay in the shallow water.

But if you want to catch the big fish, you gotta go deeper."

— David Lynch (quoted in the spirit of imagination)

So go deeper. Not just in your code, but in your questions.

Ask what hasn't been asked. Build what hasn't been built.

Dream what hasn't been seen.

You're not here just to remix the culture.

You're here to architect it.

Innovation ain't about invention from scratch—it's about connection.

Connect your roots to your route.

Your imagination to your implementation.

Your voice to your vision.

Because when you do?

That's when the world realizes it wasn't the degrees, the resources, or the perfect syntax holding us back.

It was the lie that we didn't belong here.

And now, that lie has expired.

CHAPTER 8: Architects of Innovation—

Imagination without application is like beats with no bars—potential without impact.

This is where we shift from dreaming to doing. But not just any doing—we vibe with purpose.

You ever notice how kids invent entire worlds with just cardboard, crayons, and conversation? That's raw imagination.

Now picture that same instinct, but paired with the tools to scale it.

That's where we are right now. In the age where dreams get documented in code.

But we don't code like they code.

We speak rhythm. We write tone. We breathe flow.

The future ain't about fitting in. It's about fitting your imagination into a system that bends with your genius.

"When the paradigm changes, the culture is going to change."-19keys

That paradigm shift? It starts with language. And when you control the language, you control the direction.

Imagination empowers you to rename what you see.

What they call "problem" you might see as "prompt."

What they define as "disadvantage" you might decode as "perspective."

That's not semantics—that's software. Mental software.

And once you rewire that, you become unstoppable.

So how do you apply this?

- Start with your story. Don't erase your roots to fit the platform.

- Think about a tool or app that could make life easier—for you or your people.
- Write the vibe of that solution. What it looks like. What it feels like. What it sounds like.

That's imagination doing data entry.

And when it gets translated into visuals, wireframes, and MVPs, guess what?

You just coded your idea into existence.

LaRussell once said, "They ain't letting us in, so we're building our own door."

That's what imagination leads to: agency.

Not waiting to be discovered. Not begging for inclusion.

Building your own reality with purpose, with tools, and with vibes.

CHAPTER 8: Architects of Innovation —

Imagination is the ancestor of revolution.

It's what Harriet had in the dark. What Malcolm saw in speeches.

What Nipsey painted in Crenshaw. What you feel every time you see something that don't exist—but know it should.

Vibe coding isn't about flexing your tech skills.

It's about fulfilling your vision.

A vision that don't ask for permission.

A vision that lives in your DNA, but now has tools to express itself.

"The future belongs to those who prepare for it today."

— Malcolm X

You're not just building products—you're building possibility.

Imagination, when it gets structured, becomes a system.

And when systems are shaped by people who were once left out of the conversation?

We don't just catch up—we leap.

That's what vibe coding is doing for the next generation.

A 14-year-old in Atlanta creating an AI-powered budgeting tool for his community.

A mother in Houston designing a wellness app using voice prompts in AAVE.

A barber in Oakland developing a scheduling system using no-code to run his entire shop.

This isn't sci-fi.

This is now.

And it all started with the imagination to believe:

- That we belong in tech.
- That our voices are valid prompts.
- That our ideas deserve platforms.

Now, let this chapter close the way we began this book—by declaring a shift:

We no longer wait for systems to invite us.

We build, code, document, and scale systems with our rhythm. Our syntax. Our swagger. Our standards.

Imagination ain't soft.

It's the core processor behind every revolution, every invention, every transformation that mattered.

So imagine boldly.

Build fluently.

And vibe like your future depends on it.

Because it does.

CHAPTER 9: THE CODE THEY NEVER TAUGHT US

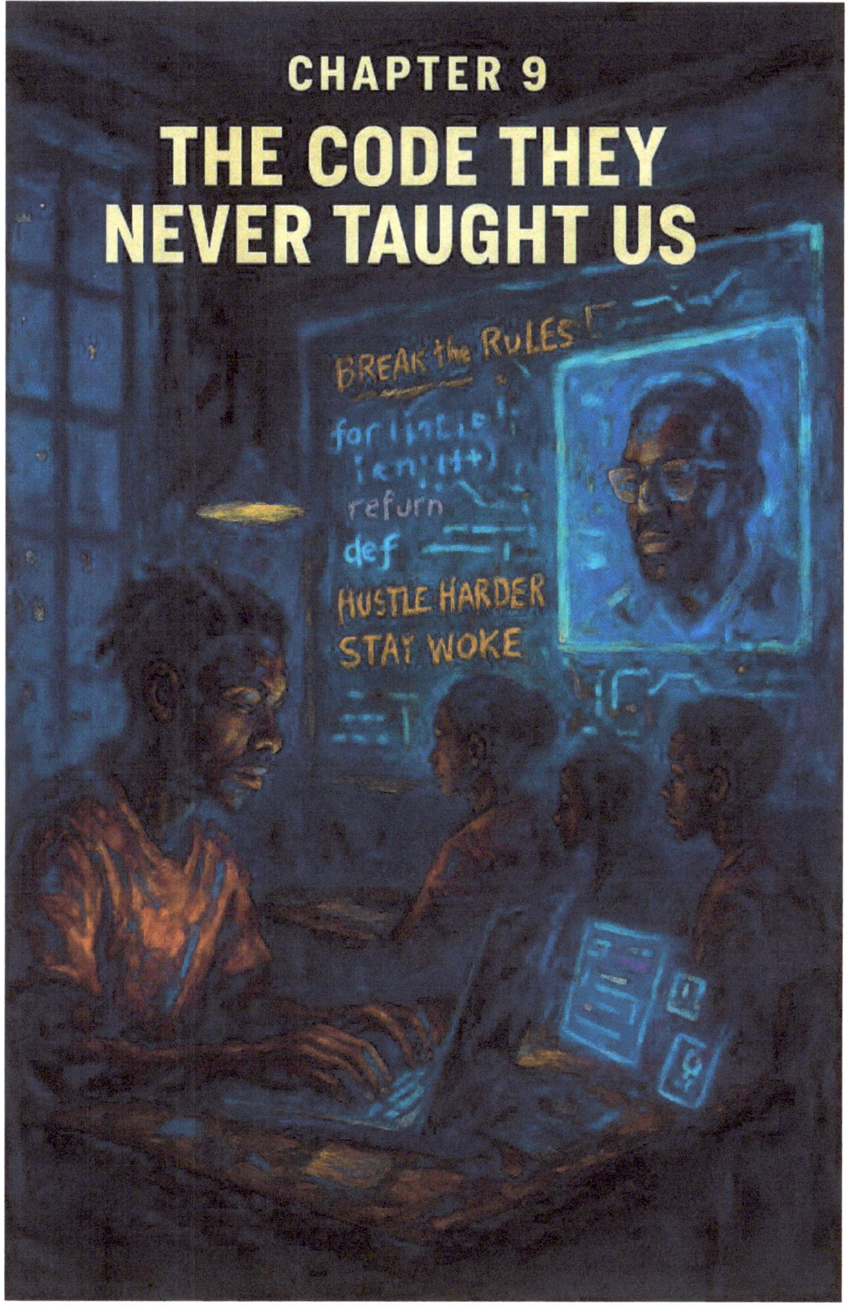
CHAPTER 9
THE CODE THEY NEVER TAUGHT US
BREAK the RULES
def
HUSTLE HARDER
STAY WOKE

CHAPTER 9: THE CODE THEY NEVER TAUGHT US

They never taught us how to write ourselves into the system.

Because the system was never built with us in mind.

They gave us instructions, but never the blueprint.

They gave us products, but not platforms.

They taught us how to download—but never how to design.

But here's the truth: we've always had the code in us.

We just didn't call it that.

It looked like storytelling.

It sounded like rhythm.

It moved like hustle.

It was system logic—just wrapped in a different syntax.

And now, in the age of AI and automation, we're waking up to the fact that our language, our mindset, our innovation—it all matters.

It's not just valuable—it's necessary.

They never taught us how to talk to machines.

So we started teaching the machines to understand us.

That's vibe coding.

Let me ask you something:

When's the last time you saw a coding class that broke down algorithms using rap battles?

Or prompt engineering explained through barbershop logic?

Or automation modeled on how we pass down wisdom in a family kitchen?

You probably haven't.

Because they didn't design this space for us.

But now we're rewriting it.

And not just through participation—through definition.

They never taught us the code because they knew what would happen when we learned to write it ourselves.

We'd remix it.

Rebuild it.

Reshape the tech world in our image.

That's why AAVE matters.

That's why streetwear blew up.

That's why hip hop birthed billionaires.

Culture is code.

And when you begin to see yourself—not just as a consumer of tech, but as an architect of experience—you shift.

You stop following rules and start writing your own protocols.

You stop trying to prove yourself and start designing systems that already know your worth.

That's what this page is about.

This ain't about fitting into their system.

This is about remembering we've always had one of our own.

It's why when we talk about vibe coding, we're not just talking tools—we're talking philosophy.

We're talking access that honors experience.

We're talking design that centers culture.

We're talking prompts that carry pain, joy, brilliance, and purpose.

We're not asking to be included—we're setting the rules.

So when they ask what we're building, you can look them dead in the eye and say:

"We're building what should've been here all along."

CHAPTER 9: THE CODE THEY NEVER TAUGHT US

We was handed manuals, but left out the parts written in our voice.

Taught the syntax but skipped the soul.

They gave us the code—but not the culture.

But we been scripting survival.

Every cipher, every side hustle, every makeshift studio in a backroom garage?

That's engineering. That's design thinking.

That's grassroots innovation in real time.

The tech world wants clean code—but we come with lived complexity.

And that's not a flaw. That's the feature.

See, we're not here to memorize methods—we're here to remix them.

We apply pressure like a function.

We loop resilience.

We debug oppression daily.

And here's what they don't get:

You can't teach culture like it's a plug-in.

You gotta live it.

You gotta feel the rhythm of it in your work.

When we build, we build with meaning.

Our interfaces aren't just user-friendly—they're people-powered.

Our outputs don't just serve—they inspire.

Because our inputs are stories, language, heritage.

The code they never taught us?
It's embedded in our instinct.
It's knowing the difference between data and truth.
Between access and equity.
Between being included—and being the blueprint.
We don't need permission to innovate.
We just need space to create.
And now? We're claiming it.
Line by line. Build by build. Prompt by prompt.
They never handed us the whole curriculum—
But we're writing our own textbook.
Right now.

CHAPTER 9: THE CODE THEY NEVER TAUGHT US

This game wasn't built with us in mind—
But somehow, we still mastered the controls.
We learned by watching.
By listening.
By testing keys like MPC pads until rhythm and logic synced.
You ever notice how we take what's rigid and make it ride?
That's what we do with code.
We don't just learn it—we reimagine it.
Our approach ain't robotic—it's intuitive.
We understand flow.
We build for feel.
We architect with soul.
Most systems want you to follow the rules.
But what if the rules were written to keep you out?
That's where vibe coding steps in.
Because here's the truth:
What they teach in bootcamps don't match what we know in barbershops.
What they praise in think tanks, we been building in basements.
That DIY mentality? It's always been our default setting.
We improvise solutions.
We create new languages.
We make frameworks out of necessity.
And while the world races to perfect artificial intelligence,
we've been perfecting cultural intelligence.

Real intelligence.

The kind you can't copy-paste.

You know what's more valuable than lines of code?

Lines of truth.

Lines of vision.

Lines that free our people from just consuming tech to commanding it.

Because when we write code that reflects who we are?

We write freedom.

We ain't just learning how to code apps.

We're learning how to code liberation.

CHAPTER 9: THE CODE THEY NEVER TAUGHT US

They taught us syntax, but not system design.
Variables, but not vision.
Loops, but not liberation.
That's the gap we're closing.
Because tech isn't just about commands—it's about context.
It's about knowing your user, your environment, your rhythm.
And let's be real: who's more contextual than us?
We've been writing code in our culture for generations.
Our slang evolves faster than software updates.
Our fashion reprograms the runway.
Our music? That's data moving the soul.
So how do we bring that into the tech stack?
By building like we talk.
By designing like we dance.
By structuring like we storytell.
Vibe coding is the intersection of identity and intention.
It's not a methodology. It's a movement.
A blueprint where intuition sits beside instruction.
You want proof?
Look at Black Twitter—it's an algorithm of expression.
Look at Verzuz—it's UX and culture in a sound clash.
Look at how we flipped Clubhouse into town halls.
We take the tool and remix the rule.
That's the part they don't teach you.
How to take a GitHub repo and turn it into a gospel.

How to convert Python into poetry.

How to turn API access into ancestral power.

This page of the book?

It ain't about fitting in.

It's about rewriting the manual.

Because when we code from our core,

We don't need permission—we build platforms that make space.

This isn't about "diversity in tech." Diversity is them asking if we'd like to sit at the table. Dominion is us owning the building. We are no longer fitting into someone else's operating system—we are writing the kernel from scratch.

And let's be clear: this is economic. Fintech apps that actually account for lived experience. Blockchain contracts that lock in value where traditional banks shut doors. DAOs that decentralize not just governance, but dignity.

This page isn't about fitting in. It's about authoring the manual.

Because when we build from our core, no one can evict us from what we've created. Platforms born of permission are fragile. Platforms born of power? They're permanent.

We're not just coding to solve problems. We're coding to shape futures. And once you realize that—once you see the blueprint hidden in your own rhythm—you stop waiting for the next big thing.

You become it.

CHAPTER 9: THE CODE THEY NEVER TAUGHT US

This is where the curtain gets pulled back.

You were never supposed to read this kind of book.

Not like this. Not with this tone. Not with this truth.

But here you are, decoding what they kept gated.

Because they didn't want us to know that coding could feel like composing. That product design could come from project hallways. That UX could be inspired by the way your cousin tells stories at the cookout. But now we know better.

This page isn't about protest—it's about blueprint.

The kind that fits your voice. Your neighborhood. Your tempo.

We're building from scratch—but not from nothing. We're building from culture.

The late-night cipher becomes data flow. The chopped & screwed beat becomes layered architecture.

The barbershop debate becomes rapid prototyping. They never taught us code because they didn't want us building.

They knew once we started constructing tech in our image—

Their image would start looking limited.

We don't just need diversity in tech. We need dominion in creation. The lesson now is this:

Don't wait for validation. Build like your culture already has it. Because it does.

They taught us to debug syntax errors.

We're teaching each other to debug systemic gaps.

That's the revolution. You want to be a vibe coder? Start where you are. Use your language.

Trust your rhythm. Design for your people.

Because the real power in code ain't the computer.

It's the consciousness behind it.

Got it , get it , Good.

The truth is, once we start embedding our values into the logic of these systems, the economy changes. No more waiting for loans denied by algorithms that never understood us. No more being data points in someone else's empire. When we build decentralized finance with our hands, our heads, and our heart, we take dominion over the flow of capital.

This ain't just theory. This is blueprint.

- Fintech apps that speak our language of survival and strategy.
- Credit models that count hustle and community trust as metrics of value.
- DAOs that move like digital cooperatives, where ownership is shared and decisions are collective.
- Blockchain systems that don't just tokenize assets but tokenize legacy—land, culture, creativity.

The revolution is in building an economy where our rhythm sets the terms. Where our code becomes the contract. Where our vibe is the validator.

So let's be clear: the next wave of builders aren't just coders. They're architects of freedom. The future bankers, but without the banks. The future policymakers, but without the red tape. The future economists, but without the gatekeepers.

This page isn't just about apps—it's about autonomy. About reclaiming the keys to systems that told us we could only be users, never authors.

CHAPTER 10: TWELVE VIBE LAWS: URBAN PROTOCOLS FOR

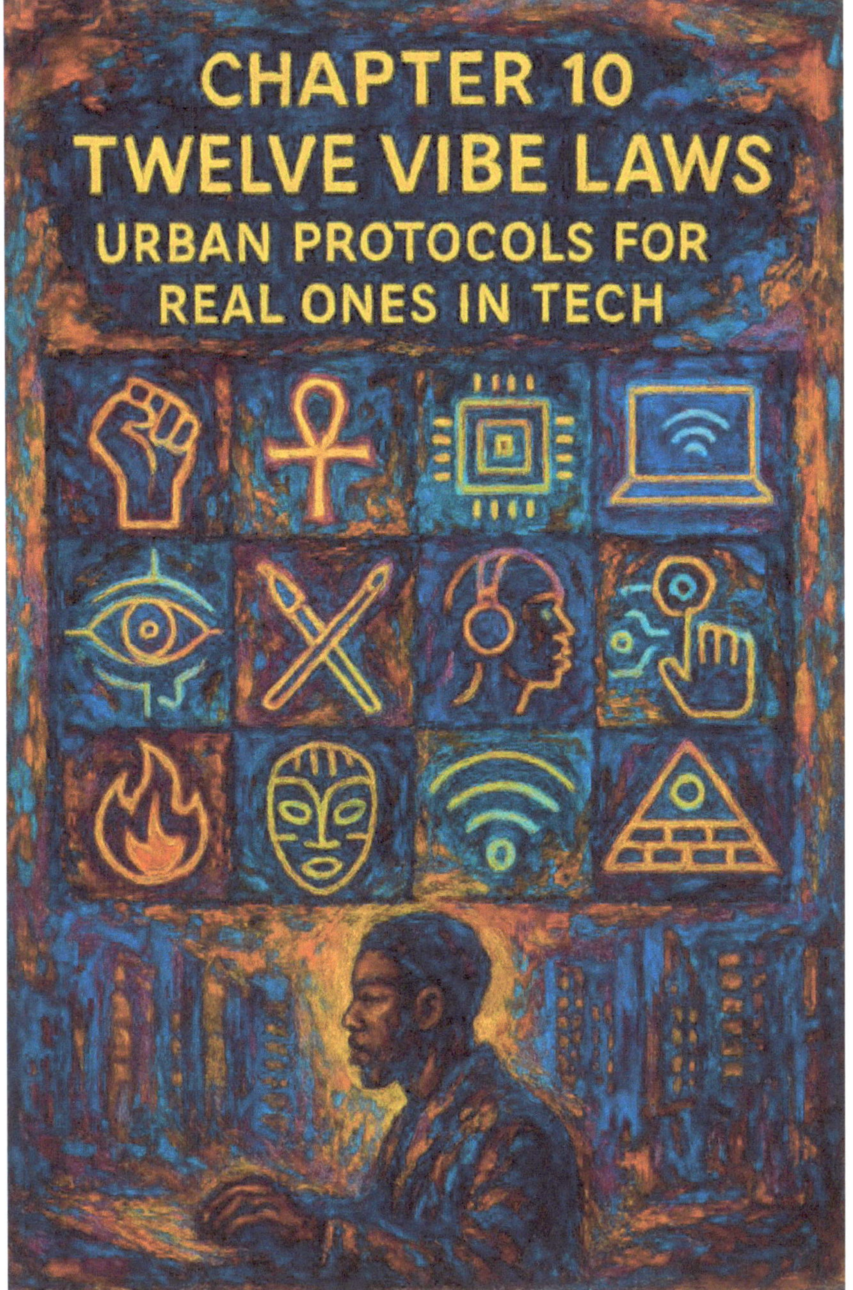
CHAPTER 10
TWELVE VIBE LAWS
URBAN PROTOCOLS FOR
REAL ONES IN TECH

CHAPTER 10: TWELVE VIBE LAWS: PROTOCOLS FOR REAL O

You ever notice how real game don't come from a classroom?

It comes from the block. From barbershop debates. From that OG who pulled you aside and said, "Yo, move smarter." Vibe coding moves the same way—it's not just about clean syntax and pretty apps. It's about knowing the terrain, understanding the energy, and coding with your soul, not just your skills.

This chapter ain't about rigid rules—it's about real ones. The type of laws you learn after messing up, winning big, and watching close.

We call them the **Twelve Vibe Laws.** They're not corny

"best practices." They're protocols. Urban truths. The codes behind the code.

These are survival skills, not study guides.

And we breaking it down so you can build better, move smarter, and stay fly in the process.

Let's start with the first four:

1. Keep Your Stack Simple

If your tech stack looking like a Jenga tower ready to fall—you already lost. Simple ain't lazy. Simple is smart. Use tools that vibe with you. Keep what works. Drop the rest.

"Too many apps don't make you efficient. They make you overwhelmed."

2. Talk to AI Like It's Your Partner

Don't treat AI like it's magic. Talk to it with purpose. Give it clear roles, tone, and context. Don't say "write a blog." Say "act as a brand strategist and write a blog for a sneaker drop aimed at Gen Z with a poetic tone." See the difference?

3. Ask for Options, Not Perfection

Real creatives don't look for the "right" answer. They look for flavor. When you prompt AI, ask for versions. Samples. Vibes. Then remix what works. That's how you find your voice in the noise.

4. Break Big Things Into Little Pieces

Every big idea got a bunch of small moves under it. Don't ask AI to build an empire in one shot. Break it down. "Write the intro." "Now outline the features." "Now give me a script." Step by step—like building a hook before the verse.

You feel that energy?

That's what this chapter is built on.

No gatekeeping. No tech snobbery. Just pure, uncut coding wisdom that fits your hustle.

CHAPTER 10: TWELVE VIBE LAWS: PROTOCOLS FOR REAL O

Let's keep it rollin'.

You got the first four vibe laws in your bag. Now we expand the blueprint. These next four ain't about looking smart—they about moving different. Precise. Intentional. Urban tech protocol.

You ain't just building code. You building how people feel when they interact with what you create.

So let's dig in:

5. Give the Code Context

AI is smart—but not psychic. If you don't feed it the world it's working in, don't expect it to create something that lives in yours. Give it the vibe, the backstory, the slang, the stakes. Context is your GPS.

"The more your input feels like your reality, the more the output reflects your vision."

6. Test Like You Got Enemies

Every real one knows—you don't just trust something 'cause it looks good. You test it. You poke it. You hit every angle like someone tryna break in. Your code gotta survive real-world chaos. Be ruthless. Be paranoid. That's love.

7. Don't Marry the First Draft

We don't do ego in vibe coding. Fall in love with the process, not the product. If it don't slap? Scrap it. Tweak it. Ask AI again. Reimagine the frame. Don't be afraid to hit the reset button. You ain't stuck—you're sculpting.

8. Use Your Voice, Not Just Your Fingers

Talk your code into existence. Literally. Use voice prompts. Speak your flow. Let your tone guide the rhythm. When you use your voice, you start building with soul. AI ain't just reading your words—it's reading your energy.

These ain't tips. These are survival manuals. This is how you stay sharp in a digital world that moves fast and forgets faster. Each law ain't just about how to use AI—it's how to stay you in the process.

CHAPTER 10: TWELVE VIBE LAWS: PROTOCOLS FOR REAL O

You've made it this far because you're not just interested in tech—you're determined to flip it your way. That's what these next four Vibe Laws are about. Staying real while scaling smart.

The streets taught us survival. Now we apply that wisdom to creation.

Let's get into Laws 9 through 12:

9. Break It Down, Don't Break Your Spirit

If it feels too big, it probably is. That don't mean it ain't worth doing—it means break it into pieces. Small steps. Bite-sized moves. Chop the mission into mini-wins. One vibe at a time builds momentum. That's how we build anything lasting.

"Chunk the chaos. Stack the steps. Get to the vibe without the burnout."

10. Control the Version, Control the Vision

Use version control. That's not just GitHub—it's a mindset. Know where your idea started. Track how it evolves. Archive the missteps. Document the glow-ups. That's history in the making. That's how we preserve the roots while building the future.

11. Let the Code Teach You Back

Don't just make AI spit code—make it explain the "why." Let it walk you through the logic, the structure, the flow. Learn while you build.

Turn your prompts into mentors. The more you understand, the doper your tweaks become.

12. Design for Your People

If the final product don't vibe with your fam, your hood, your community—it missed the mark. Build tools your auntie can use. Platforms your little cousin can flex with. Make your creations culturally fluent and functionally tight.

"When your tech speaks their language, they don't just use it—they trust it."And that's the code.

Twelve Vibe Laws. Not for clout but for clarity. For power. For liberation.

CHAPTER 10: TWELVE VIBE LAWS: PROTOCOLS 4 REAL1's

Let's be real—most tech playbooks weren't written with us in mind. That's why we had to flip the language. Remix the methods. Build a protocol that feels like us and works for us.

The Twelve Vibe Laws ain't just a checklist—they're cultural tech commandments.

They remind us that coding isn't neutral. That prompts ain't just prompts. That algorithms reflect assumptions—and we got the power to challenge that.

They say "move fast and break things." We say "move with purpose and build what lasts."

These laws are protection.

They're blueprint and boundary.

They tell you:

• You ain't gotta sound like them to build like you.

• You don't need validation from the valley to innovate from your block.

• You don't have to sacrifice your dialect, your swag, or your story to be heard in the digital space.

That's the lesson.

We're not coding to conform—we're coding to create.

And when we use these Vibe Laws, we:

• Simplify complex tools

• Turn culture into functionality

• Center the user experience in rhythm, not rigidity

You now have the strategy to build in your own frequency.

CHAPTER 10: TWELVE VIBE LAWS: PROTOCOLS 4 Real 1's

So let's run it back.

We didn't just write a book—we built a blueprint.

We kicked things off with vision—where tech meets soul, where imagination is the foundation. We said let the creators create, gave power back to the storytellers, the builders, the ones who never got the manual but built anyway.

We broke down the codes they never taught us. We reminded the block that algorithms can reflect us when we inject our rhythm into the syntax. We showed that vibe coding ain't just about what you build—but how you build, why you build, and who you're building it for.

We brought culture to code. We flipped the language of prompt engineering and turned it into a cipher. We said your swag matters in digital spaces. That your hustle, your roots, your rhythm—that's data, too. That's value.

We told you to imagine wildly. To architect futures from the bottom up. To remember that Black brilliance has always hacked systems—from cotton fields to code bases. From mixtapes to machine learning.

And then we handed you these Twelve Vibe Laws—real rules for real ones. Not rules to restrict, but to guide. To uplift. To help you move through this new digital world without losing yourself.

This ain't the end.

It's the beginning of a new code. One that starts in the heart, travels through the mind, and manifests in every line, every app, every idea you drop.

You got the keys now.

Vibe coding is no longer theory. It's your toolkit.

So what are you building?

Because the future ain't waiting.

It's NOW!!!

CHAPTER 11 — Bridging the Digital Divide

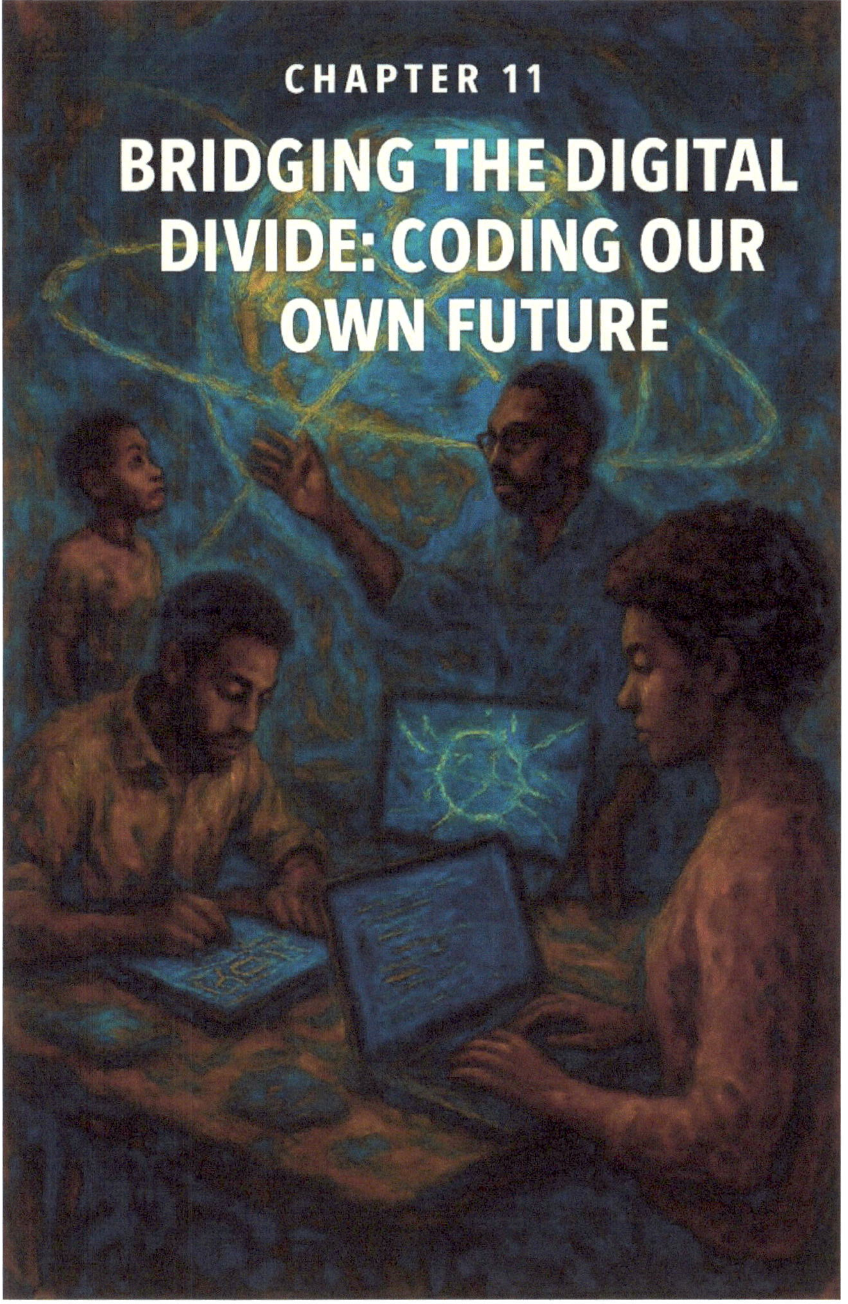
CHAPTER 11
BRIDGING THE DIGITAL DIVIDE: CODING OUR OWN FUTURE

CHAPTER 11 – Bridging the Digital Divide: Coding O

The Interface Is Not Neutral

You ever used a platform and felt like it didn't know you—didn't see you? That wasn't an accident. That was design.

Tech doesn't just happen. It's made. Every dropdown menu, every facial recognition model, every AI output—we're not just looking at tools. We're looking at someone else's worldview written in code. And more often than not, that worldview wasn't built with us in mind.

There's this myth in tech: that code is neutral, that algorithms are objective, that design is about functionality alone. But let's be clear—design is political. It shapes who gets seen, who gets heard, and who gets help.

Take facial recognition. If it can't read dark skin properly, it's not just a bug—it's a bias. When loan algorithms deny credit based on zip codes tied to redlining, that's not innovation—it's inherited injustice. When health tools underdiagnose because they weren't trained on our bodies, we're not being overlooked—we're being excluded.

That's why this page starts with a warning, and a truth:

"You may not take an interest in AI, but AI will take an interest in you."

Whether we engage or not, these systems are being trained, deployed, and enforced in our lives every day. The question is—are we shaping them, or are they shaping us?

And this is where the conversation shifts from critique to power. Because the antidote to exclusion is creation. The answer to bias is building. If tech is the language of tomorrow, then learning to speak it fluently—on our own terms—becomes survival.

But it's more than just learning Python or deploying a bot. It's about ownership of the interface. About embedding our culture into the code, our values into the variables. Because until we write ourselves into the tech, we're at the mercy of those who wrote us out.

So this isn't just about learning to code. It's about learning to see code as culture. As an extension of narrative. As a mirror.

Because here's the hard truth: when tech doesn't reflect us, it rewrites us.

That's why bridging the digital divide isn't about bandwidth alone—it's about belief. The belief that we belong not just on the internet, but in the infrastructure. That our problems, our dialects, our dreams deserve to be centered in every interface.

And that's how we code a future worth living in.

CHAPTER 11 – Bridging the Digital Divide: Coding O

That's how we code a future worth living in.

And when we do, we stop just consuming the digital—we begin designing it. That's the real shift. Not just clicking through the world, but crafting it. Not just scrolling someone else's imagination, but publishing our own.

Because here's the quiet revolution: we're no longer just users. We're becoming creators.

You feel that moment when the spark hits? When you realize that every system, every feature, every screen you've ever tapped was built by someone no smarter than you? That's when the myth of tech being "not for us" falls apart. That's when the gears start turning.

I met a sister from Newark who swore she wasn't "technical." She said, "I just do hair, manage my dad's barbershop schedule, and run a nail page on Instagram." I said, "You don't realize that's UX design, flow optimization, and brand development. You've been coding with culture—you just didn't call it that."

See, we've been creating systems out of survival since day one. The block is just the original network. The barbershop is our first data hub. The kitchen table? That's where we've always done real strategy. So when people say, "Tech feels foreign," what they really mean is, "Tech has never felt like mine."

But it is. It always has been.

And once we stop waiting for permission to innovate, we start innovating with purpose. We stop looking at code as a barrier and start seeing it as a beat—a rhythm we've already mastered.

Because the minute you understand you can build, you stop accepting what's built for you. You stop adapting to broken systems and start crafting systems that adapt to your people.

That's the shift—from consumer to creator.

It don't come with a fancy badge or a new degree. It comes with a moment. A realization. A vibe. It comes when someone tells you, "You don't have to just be a user of tech. You can be the one who defines it."

That moment is liberation. That moment is blueprint. That moment is your cue to create.

And creation? It's not a luxury—it's a necessity. Especially when the systems we rely on were never meant to reflect our truth.

So here's the call: Build something only you could imagine. Something that feels like your block, your story, your soul. Because when tech speaks your language, it doesn't just work—it welcomes.

And that's when you know you've stepped into authorship. That's when you know the interface is finally listening.

CHAPTER 11 — Bridging the Digital Divide: Coding O

By the time we start creating our own tools, our next question should be: why not build the brains behind the tools too?

Because it's not just about having access to AI—it's about authorship over intelligence itself.

Language models shape reality. They finish your sentences, predict your searches, generate your images, and even respond like they know your soul. But here's the kicker—they don't know you. They were never trained on your voice, your slang, your grandmother's wisdom, or your community's truths. And if we don't build our own? They never will.

See, most LLMs are mirrors. But what they reflect depends on what they were fed. And right now, most of them were trained on data that don't sound like us, look like us, or think like us. So when we ask them for answers, they give us reflections of systems that have already failed us.

That's why building our own models isn't a flex—it's a form of self-defense.

Because when you control the lens, you control the language. And when you control the language, you shape the logic.

There's a line I heard once that hit different:

"The most dangerous skill in the world is coming up with the ideal."

Think about that. Not the code, not the pitch deck—the ideal. The vision. The blueprint. Because whoever holds the ideal, holds the future.

And that's why our ideas need systems. Not just spoken out loud in living rooms, but encoded into algorithms. Trained into tools. Scaled into services.

We got elders who've been solving systems with stories for generations. Now imagine training an LLM on those stories. Imagine a model that doesn't just know data—but knows diaspora. That can parse Black English with fluency. That doesn't autocorrect our culture out of existence.

We need tools that don't just understand what we say—but why we say it.

Because this ain't about AI being "woke." It's about AI being rooted. Rooted in our reality. Rooted in our rhythm. Rooted in our respect for nuance and neighborhood.

The future of intelligence can't be outsourced.

So if we're serious about bridging the digital divide, we can't just be content logging in—we need to start logging legacy. Building brains that reflect our truth. Constructing systems that understand our soul.

And to do that, we must become the architects of thought itself.

CHAPTER 11 – Bridging the Digital Divide: Coding O

It's not enough to show up online—we've got to show out with intention.

Because bridging the digital divide? It's not just about handing out laptops and hoping something sticks. That's charity. What we need is clarity. We need fluency. We need frameworks that fit the realities of our people.

The real gap isn't in tools—it's in trust. It's in translation. It's in the belief that the hood can house a hacker, that a grandmother in Baton Rouge can become an app designer, that a teenager in the Bronx can teach prompt engineering on Twitch.

That belief doesn't come from bandwidth. It comes from proof. From seeing someone who looks like you build something that changes lives.

We're not waiting for that change to trickle down. We're writing it into existence—one prompt, one prototype, one platform at a time.

That's why vibe coding matters. It doesn't just teach syntax—it teaches sovereignty. It shows people that tech isn't this cold corporate tower you have to beg your way into. It's a canvas. A cipher. A cipher where your life becomes the logic.

One student once told me, *"I don't think in code, I think in sneakers."*

I asked him what he meant. He broke down how he tracks release dates, flips pairs, and studies resale value.

I told him, *"That's inventory management, that's market analysis, that's data forecasting. All you have to do is digitize what you already do."*

You don't force folks into tech—**you translate tech into them.**

And once they feel that first "Hello World" moment, once they see the screen talk back in a voice they understand? That's when the bridge is built—not from one side to another, but from within.

This isn't about assimilation—it's about amplification. We don't need to fit into tech. Tech needs to stretch to fit us. It needs to hold our stories, honor our data, and follow our lead.

Because when you give someone the tools and the truth, you don't just close the gap—you close the grip. You help them hold their future with both hands.

That's what bridging really means.

But we also have to remember: every design decision shapes social inequities. The way interfaces are built, the way algorithms are trained, the way policies get coded into platforms—all of it either expands opportunity or enforces oppression. Code is never neutral; it carries the fingerprints of its creators.

And for too long, the creative imagination has been colonized—pulled between chaos and clarity, stolen and resold to us in fragments. We've seen what happens when our cultural genius is extracted, remixed, and monetized without ever being credited. That's not inclusion—that's extraction.

This is what I call *predatorial inclusion*: when institutions open the door just wide enough for excluded groups to walk through, but impose biased terms, hidden costs, or exploitative conditions as the price of admission. Access becomes another trap. Validation becomes another leash.

The fight for true power isn't just about who codes—it's about who gets to imagine. The real battleground is imagination itself.

Because whoever controls the imagination controls the infrastructure of tomorrow.

The fight for the future is, at its core, a fight over who is allowed to dream it today.

So how do we bridge the gap? That question has always lived with us, from the plantation fields to the projects, from the block to the blockchain. And the answer is the same now as it's always been: we build, we reclaim, and we refuse to wait for permission.

CHAPTER 11 – Bridging the Digital Divide

Bridging the digital divide has never been about plugging cords into sockets—it's about plugging people back into power.

See, folks love to act like access alone is the answer. Pass out some Chromebooks, throw Wi-Fi in a neighborhood, and boom—problem solved. But access without alignment is just noise. It's not that our people don't have brilliance—it's that the system keeps trying to hand us tools without context, platforms without pathways.

The divide isn't measured in megabytes—it's measured in mindsets. It's the difference between someone seeing a phone as just a way to scroll versus seeing it as a studio, a classroom, a bank, a printing press, a world-building engine. That shift doesn't come from a download. It comes from translation. From trust. From someone showing you that the same creativity you use to stretch a dollar or flip a hustle is the same creativity that powers algorithms.

That's the work: not just introducing new tech, but introducing new truths.

Because let's keep it real—when tech has been built without us, it's failed us. Every single time. Whether it's predictive policing apps coded with bias or platforms designed to monetize our culture without ever crediting the creators, we've seen what exclusion looks like in code. And we refuse to be written out of the next version.

That's why vibe coding matters. Because vibe coding is about taking the genius already alive in the hood, in the barbershops, in the beauty salons, in the after-school cyphers—and reframing it as engineering. It's about reminding a young queen who sells lip gloss online that she's already running e-commerce, that her Shopify store is as valid as any startup pitch deck. It's about showing a young king who DJs block parties that he's already a systems designer—curating data, mixing patterns, scaling vibes.

This isn't charity. This is clarity.

When someone finally sees themselves as more than just a user, more than just a consumer—as a *builder*—that's when the ground shifts. That's when you don't just bridge the gap, you burn the blueprint that said the gap had to exist in the first place.

And here's the key: the bridge we're building isn't one-way. It doesn't just lead our people into tech—it forces tech to walk toward us too. To meet us where we live, in our rhythm, in our language, in our stories.

Because tech without culture is cold. Culture without tech is capped. But when code and culture fuse? That's when we get something unstoppable.

Bridging the divide isn't just about closing distance—it's about opening destiny. It's about making sure our fingerprints are on the future, not just our data.

As Iddris Sandu reminds us: *"If I'm getting credit from a biased platform that wasn't built for me, where does that get me? Because credit means validation."*

That's why we don't just want credit—we want creation. Not validation, but valuation. A future that's not borrowed, but built by us.

The real flex ain't just knowing how to use the system—it's knowing how to design one that speaks your name.

This is about more than coding apps or prompting AI. It's about understanding that we hold the blueprint. That every scroll, every share, every build becomes an artifact of intention. A piece of digital resistance. A tool for transformation.

When we talk about coding our own future, we're not just talking about careers—we're talking about continuity. About making sure our culture don't get lost in translation. About making sure that when the next generation opens a laptop, they don't just see the web—they see themselves.

Because if we don't design the data, someone else decides the destiny.

I've seen what happens when Black brilliance gets behind the keyboard—apps that heal, platforms that teach, systems that feel like home. That's what it looks like when we stop asking to be included and start demanding that the code reflects the collective.

It's not just innovation—it's a love letter to the ones who were told they didn't belong here.

So what comes next?

We teach each other. We fund each other. We build slow, deep, and rooted. We normalize labs in libraries, startup convos in salons, and code reviews in barbershops. We build tech that doesn't erase us—but remembers us. Honors us. Extends us.

That's the next chapter of vibe coding. Not just ownership. Legacy.

Because the digital divide doesn't end when everyone logs on. It ends when everyone logs in to themselves. When they know they're not just navigating a system—they're authors of it.

So here's what I leave you with:

Build that tool. Teach that skill. Share that prompt. Start that idea.

Even if it's messy. Even if it's incomplete. Even if no one claps at first.

Because every build is a bridge.

Every prompt is a prayer.

Every app is a heartbeat from the culture that birthed it.

And the future? It's not waiting.

It's being written right now.

In our language.

On our terms.

With our vibe.

So don't let this just be something you read. Let it be something you move on.

Here's what you do next:

• Pick a problem in your life or community. Doesn't matter how big or small. Write it down.

• Prompt it. Describe it like you're explaining it to an AI that can help you solve it. That's your first blueprint.

• Prototype it. Use what you've got—pen and paper, Canva, Replit, Glide. Doesn't have to be perfect. Just has to be real.

• Share it. With a homie, a teacher, a cousin. Let the idea breathe.

• Build again. Every prompt sharpens your power. Every attempt deepens your understanding. Keep moving.

And when you're ready to go further?

Come build with us at www.UniverseCity.ai — the place where creators become coders, storytellers become system designers, and culture becomes code.

You don't need to be perfect.

You just need to be present.

The future is wide open—

and now that you've got the blueprint,

it's time to start building.

Come learn more. Come build what's next.

Glossary

Here's an expanded Glossary section with more terms explained in a culturally resonant and tech-savvy voice:

◈ GLOSSARY: VIBE CODING TERMS (EXTENDED) PAGE

1. **Vibe Coding** – Programming with flavor. Your style, your story, your syntax. A new way to make tech feel like home.
2. **Prompt Engineering** – Giving AI game. It's not just what you ask—it's how you ask it, with intention and swagger.
3. **Stack** – Your tech toolbox. It's what you use to build—from code to coffee.
4. **API** – A plug. It lets different apps talk like homies at a cypher.
5. **No-Code Tools** – Drag, drop, done. Tech building without the stress.
6. **Syntax** – Code's grammar rules. Miss a bracket, and your whole set gets shut down.
7. **Digital Fluency** – Tech with fluency and finesse. Understanding tools like it's second nature.
8. **AAVE** – African American Vernacular English. The original algorithm of cool. Valid in life and in code.
9. **Workflow** – The way you move from idea to execution. Your studio session, your rhythm.
10. **Version Control** – The timeline. Track edits, rollbacks, and every change you ever made.
11. **Debugging** – Fixing what's broken. Like squashing rumors—but in your code.

12. **Frontend** – What users see. The face of your app. Make it clean, make it vibey.

13. **Backend** – What runs behind the scenes. It's the engine under the hood.

14. **Algorithm** – A recipe. A set of steps that delivers a result. Whether it's dinner or TikTok recommendations.

15. **Deployment** – Going live. Your code's first concert—mic check included.

16. **Responsive Design** – Code that adapts to the screen. Whether it's a phone, tablet, or your cousin's cracked laptop.

17. **Open Source** – Tech for the people, by the people. Anyone can use, remix, and build on it.

18. **Data Bias** – When the algorithm doesn't see you right. That's why representation in tech matters.

19. **Command Line** – Text-only interface. The old school terminal that still holds serious power.

20. **Hackathon** – Code battles. 24-48 hours of building, breaking, and bonding.

21. **Machine Learning** – When AI learns patterns like your grandma learning your favorite dish from memory.

22. **Tokenization** – Breaking things down into bite-sized pieces. Useful in security and linguistics.

23. **UI / UX** – User Interface and Experience. How something looks and how it feels.

24. **Encryption** – Locking your digital secrets. Like writing in code only you understand.

25. **Cloud** – Data floating in cyberspace. Your files, anywhere, anytime.

Here are more Glossary terms added to deepen the understanding and make the culture-tech fusion even stronger:

———

GLOSSARY: VIBE CODING TERMS (EXTENDED CONTINUED) PAGE

26. **Sandbox** – A safe space to experiment. Build, break, rebuild—without messing up the real thing.

27. **Iteration** – Repetition with purpose. You remix, refine, and repeat until it hits right.

28. **Wireframe** – The sketch. Like drafting bars before you lay them down in the booth.

29. **Script** – A mini program. Handles repetitive tasks like a hustler on automation.

30. **Framework** – Your foundation. Like Air Force 1s to an outfit—solid, supportive, and stylish.

31. **Runtime** – When code actually runs. It's showtime for your app.

32. **Bug** – An error in your code. The digital version of a mic drop—when you didn't mean to.

33. **Scalability** – Can it grow with you? Like turning your side hustle into a franchise.

34. **Plugin** – A feature you can install. Like adding rims to a ride—it boosts the experience.

35. **Latency** – Delay in data. Like when your Wi-Fi lags mid-FaceTime.

36. **Modular Code** – Code built in pieces. Think Lego bricks: flexible, reusable, and easy to stack.

37. **Script Kiddie** – Someone who uses code they don't understand. Ain't no respect in that.

38. **AI Model** – The brain of the machine. It learns, predicts, and responds—like a virtual sensei.

39. **Deployment Pipeline** – Your launch strategy. From the lab to the world in clean steps.

40. **Responsive Grid** – A layout system. Makes sure your site doesn't look wack on mobile.

41. **DevOps** – The bridge between development and operations. Builders and fixers in harmony.

42. **State Management** – Keeping your app's memory right. Like remembering who you texted and what was said.

43. **Event Listener** – Waits for action. Like your app's security guard—ready to react.

44. **Rendering** – Drawing stuff on the screen. Like a paintbrush but coded.

45. **CRUD** – Create, Read, Update, Delete. The four commandments of data.

46. **Callback Function** – A function waiting to be called back. Like setting up a future favor.

47. **Serverless** – Code running in the cloud with no backend babysitting.

48. **Hot Reloading** – Updating your code in real-time without refreshing. Like live DJ edits.

49. **Semantic HTML** – Clean and meaningful markup. It's your code speaking with intention.

50. **Cache** – Quick memory. Like your app remembering what you did last time—real loyal.

———

Resources

RESOURCES FOR VIBE CODERS.

These are the tools, platforms, and plug-ins that keep the vision tight and the workflow smoother than velvet. Each one helps you build with clarity, confidence, and culture. No fluff. Just function that vibes.

1. Replit – Write, run, and host code in the browser. Collaborate with your squad in real-time. No install. No delay. Just build.

2. Glide Apps – Turn your Google Sheets into clean, functional mobile apps. No coding needed. It's like creating tech with a spreadsheet twist.

3. Notion – More than just notes. Plan your projects, document your logic, and organize your coding hustle—all in one canvas.

4. ChatGPT / GPTs – Your AI co-pilot. From writing clean code to sparking new ideas, this tool's your creative partner and problem-solver.

5. Figma – Design like a pro. Whether it's a wireframe, mockup, or full UI, Figma's where your vision becomes visual.

6. GitHub – Home for your code. Track every change, team up with others, and flex your digital portfolio in public or private.

7. Canva – Logos, slides, branding, and social content—fast. Bring that clean aesthetic to your visuals without needing Photoshop.

8. Zapier – Connect your favorite apps and automate your flows. Whether it's emails, forms, or file drops—set it and forget it.

9. Tally.so – Collect data with smooth, stylish forms. Perfect for feedback, surveys, or signups—no extra tech headache.

10. Framer – Build animated websites that move and feel next-level. Visual builder, code-optional, drip-heavy designs.

11. Bolt.AI – Build ideas faster with this collaborative AI tool. Great for brainstorming, prompting, and turning sparks into scripts.

12. Tabnine – AI that predicts and completes your code. Speeds you up like you got a mentor whispering shortcuts in your ear.

13. Loveable – Design-to-code magic. Turn creative ideas into functional code with ease. Especially dope for UI-based projects.

14. Bubble – Create real web apps without typing real code. Logic, workflows, APIs—all drag and drop. Big for founders and idea heads.

15. Firebase – Get your backend right. Databases, user login, hosting—all backed by Google and made to scale.

16. n8n – Build complex automations using an intuitive visual interface. Zapier vibes, but open-source and powerful.

17. Pickaxe – Build your own GPT tools with zero code. Launch mini-AI products and personalize user flows from your prompts.

GO to https://www.UniverseCity.Ai

www.ingramcontent.com/pod-product-compliance
Ingram Content Group UK Ltd.
Pitfield, Milton Keynes, MK11 3LW, UK
UKHW060359300726
14090UKWH00001B/29

* 9 7 9 8 8 9 9 6 5 7 3 1 3 *